"Friday nights in the fall have always been special. I've had the joy of covering high school football games for 4 decades, the last 15 years in a helicopter flying throughout the mid state of Tennessee. That's a lot of schools, teams, bands, and boosters. One of my favorites has always been Blackman High School. The first time I heard their band in the stands and felt the energy and quality they generated I was so impressed that I bragged on them in our report on the game. There was a unique chemistry between the band, the fans, and the team generated by a booster club that knew how to do it 'right.' Dan Caldwell was the head of that booster club. He set the tone for the spirit and the integrity of that connection. It's been a joy to watch, though it's an art to accomplish. A booster organization can either make or break the spirit of a school. I'm delighted that he's written a book, from experience, to help booster organizations do it 'the right way.' "

– RUDY KALIS
Sports Director, WSMV-TV, Nashville, Tennessee

"In the process of raising great kids we are often thrust into roles that don't have a guidebook. *The Booster Leader* is now that desired resource for parents who are eager but untrained as booster volunteers. This is the guide that can take you from average to extraordinary in supporting your kids and their friends in a way that will leave your name as a lasting legacy."

– DAN MILLER
Author of *48 Days to the Work You Love*

"As principal of Blackman High School since 2004, and an assistant principal at anther high school since 1988, I had the opportunity to work with many booster clubs over the years. The Blackman Band Boosters were by far the most active of any in my experience, especially under the leadership of Dan Caldwell. During his tenure, many of the financial regulations from the local and federal level changed and were much more restrictive as to how boosters could operate. Where other clubs complained and some even shut down, Dan simply learned what the rules were, met with me to ensure the band boosters did things the right way, and never hesitated to continue the strong support the organization gave to our band program. Thanks to his leadership and commitment, hundreds, by now thousands of students have benefited from being a part of, in my opinion, the greatest band program in the state of Tennessee! It will benefit any booster leader to use Dan Caldwell's book as a guide for their booster organization. He has done your homework for you!"

– GAIL VICK
Principal, Blackman High School (Retired 2014)

"Through his comprehensive and meticulously detailed book, *The Booster Leader*, Dan Caldwell provides a road map to success for all volunteers and school group supporters. *The Booster Leader* functions as a great resource for the community volunteer, band director, coach, teacher, and school administrator. Supplemented by Dan's real-life experiences and examples, his book will benefit booster clubs of all shapes and sizes. A 'must read' for those desiring to get it right the first time."

– GLENN DAVIS
President, Spotlight Tours, LLC
High School Band Director (Retired)

"After an unsuccessful search for the guidebook for being an effective booster club leader, Dan Caldwell decided to create his own. In *The Booster Leader*, he demonstrates that successful and sustainable booster programs are more than a fundraising activity of popcorn, coupon books, and game programs sales. Dan provides many leadership lessons and creates a simple to follow framework for creating a solid booster organization with high integrity. By following Dan's lead, future booster leaders and volunteers will be able to focus on transforming their children's lives instead of perpetually reinventing the booster wheel."

– BILL KRUEGER
Chairman, JATCO Americas

"As the former program director of a listener-supported radio station, I know how important a solid group of volunteers can be to an organization's success. I can't count the number of times one of our staff, with no prior experience leading a group of volunteers, was thrust into a situation requiring them to do just that. Oh how I wish we had this book back then. *The Booster Leader* is the field guide we were missing."

Creator & Host, the Read to Lead Podcast
Award-winning Broadcaster

"To compete in today's challenging, global economy, businesses need competent, well-rounded employees. Dan Caldwell realizes the important role that extracurricular activities play in preparing the next generation of employees. In *The Booster Leader*, he equips passionate parent volunteers with an actionable, easy-to-implement blueprint that will provide students outstanding extracurricular opportunities. This is a 'must read' for anyone who wants to make a significant impact for years to come."

– CATHERINE GLOVER
President, Tennessee Chamber of Commerce & Industry
Tennessee Manufacturers Association

THE
BOOSTER
LEADER

35 LEADERSHIP ESSENTIALS FOR A THRIVING BOOSTER ORGANIZATION

DAN CALDWELL

Published by The Regen Group, LLC
2441-Q Old Fort Parkway #361
Murfreesboro, Tennessee 37128

ISBN 978-0-9904761-0-8
eBook ISBN 978-0-9904761-1-5

The Regen Group, LLC
MURFREESBORO, TENNESSEE

CONTENTS

To Katrina, Grant, and Katelyn.
You are my inspiration.

FOREWORD

I am absolutely thrilled to share how this book came about. My name is Brenda Monson and I have been a band director for almost 20 years. I have teaching experience at all levels: elementary school, middle school, high school, and college. Throughout my career I have had the pleasure of working with many parents. As a parent myself, I have also been involved with parent groups from the reverse side. Through my experience and relationships, I have seen, heard about, and witnessed booster organizations that were weak and unsuccessful. Likewise, I have had the pleasure of working with strong, supportive, and successful booster organizations. Each has its own dynamic, its own set of values, and each changes year to year based on one thing... leadership.

Blackman High School opened its doors in 2000 and with that, the Blaze Band was born. From the beginning of our history, the band was surrounded with awesome parental support. Like most bands and other student organizations, we had parents who would come and support the students in many ways: at camp, at the football games, at concerts, with uniforms, on band trips, etc. You name it – our parents were there. **Parents are the key component in any large student organization.** They are the ones who give of themselves and of their time, selflessly, so the organization can be successful. Parents have the ability to boost up an organization and make it thrive.

The Caldwells became part of the band in 2005. They were like many parents: eager to join this new organization, eager to serve, and expecting no recognition for their efforts. Over time, I got to know both Dan and Katrina as very giving people. No matter how busy life was, they made time to support the band program. Their participation varied from attending band events to participating and helping in whatever capacity was needed. Their efforts led many others to see them as role models.

When Dan first became booster president, I remember him coming to me and asking if there was a book he could read or a manual he could look at – anything that could help him succeed in this role he had just assumed. I felt awful. I had nothing to give him; nothing was written or outlined and I had not one piece of information to help guide him. But Dan learned. He asked questions, he met people, and he did what he needed to do to gain knowledge about the organization, how to lead it, and how to make it better. HE did it. How, you ask? The essential element in all this was something I could never give to Dan. It was something he had deep inside. It was his incredible love and passion for the Blackman High School Band. He was committed to serving the students.

It is true that Dan has an incredible background filled with various leadership roles and experiences. He is a senior manager for a global corporation where problem solving and business planning are part of his daily activities. Dan served in multiple leadership capacities with the Blackman High School Band Boosters (8 years), and also with the Boy Scouts of America (12 years). Dan is a true leader in every sense of the word. He is an excellent communicator, a go-getter, a do-gooder, and a person who can make things happen. If there is something Dan wants or needs to know, he will research the topic and find the answer. His mind is always running and he is always interested in how to do things more efficiently. Not only that, Dan is a team player who sees strength in numbers and talents in those around him. He is down to earth and genuinely takes an interest in everyone he meets. I have seen him wear many hats – and he is successful at them all. I have oftentimes thought to myself, *how does he do it?* and *where does he find the time?* and *how does he have so much energy?*

When Dan and Katrina's younger daughter graduated from high school and they left the program, I wondered what they would do to occupy their time, knowing that they had spent an amazing amount of time supporting the band program. I figured it was going to be some much deserved rest and relaxation; especially now both children were out of the house. Needless to say, I was mistaken. When I found out Dan had written this book I was surprised. I guess I should not have been. Dan is one of those people who just cannot sit still because he is continually thinking about how he might help someone else. Dan may have graduated from our program, but his heart was still with us. Dan was passionate about writing this book and remains passionate about helping others lead in their own organizations. This book is beneficial for all parents in booster organizations. This is the book Dan never had.

I have witnessed parents apprehensive about getting involved in organizations because they do not know what they need to do, or how they can help. That is what makes this book so great! Dan has outlined leadership positions in a parent organization and the roles they take on. He guides us through the entire year, as a timeline of possible expectations and tasks. The book can be used as a checklist for goals to set and achieve. There are strategies, ideas, benchmarks, and life lessons all rolled into one. It is the starting point of how YOU can be successful in your own organization. Dan makes the complexity of leading a booster organization seem uncomplicated and possible.

The Booster Leader is an outstanding guide, handbook, and reference manual for all booster organizations. There is simply not another book out there like it. I am proud to endorse it and thankful to have it as a resource for our program.

– BRENDA MONSON
Senior Director, Blackman High School Band

INTRODUCTION

Whether you have just accepted a leadership role in your child's booster organization or you're considering the possibility, chances are you're not quite sure what you're getting yourself into. You're full of enthusiasm and passion for the student program, but you're just not sure where to begin. Well, rest assured, you're not alone. Most of us feel that way starting out.

When I became an officer in the Blaze Band Boosters, I was beaming with enthusiasm. However, I quickly discovered how little I really knew about running a student support organization. Honestly, there were many aspects of a nonprofit where I simply did not know what I didn't know. Sure, there were some bumpy roads, but each experience seemed to prepare me for the next challenge. Before long, I was confident that I could roll up my sleeves and tackle any challenge that came my way.

John Maxwell says that everything rises and falls on leadership.[1] Booster organizations are unique in that volunteers fill every role. Therefore, I believe each organization's success is directly linked to the leader's ability to influence the volunteers around her.

I wrote this book for you, the booster leader, so that you may lead to your full potential. Here, I'll share my experiences and the leadership essentials for a thriving booster organization. I want you to succeed and to enrich your students' lives.

The book's major parts are devoted to the key leadership roles within the organization:

- **The Executive Leader** – president and vice president
- **The Finance Leader** – treasurer and bookkeeper
- **The Communications Leader** – secretary
- **The Committee Leader** – committee chairs

Regardless of your specific leadership role, you will benefit from reading all parts of the book. You will gain a complete understanding of the organization. You'll also see the interrelationships between the leadership roles.

I realize that you are in one of the busiest seasons of your life, so I designed the book to be read in short installments. Each of the thirty-four chapters addresses a specific topic, with a descriptive title for easy reference in the future. Within each chapter, you will find practical step-by-step instructions and best practices that you can immediately implement within your organization. Most topics are brought to life with actual stories and examples. Chapters end with leadership essentials, which are summarized for quick reference in appendix A.

A few key terms are used throughout the book. Here are their definitions:

- **Extracurricular program, or simply "program."** The students' extracurricular activity.
- **Booster organization, or "organization."** The group of parents, alumni, and community members, known as the "boosters," that support the student program.
- **Instructor.** The teacher, coach, music director, arts instructor, ROTC instructor, or other school employee who oversees the student program.

- **Executive team.** The booster organization's leadership team, comprised primarily of elected officers and the instructor(s).
- **Blaze Band Boosters.** The band boosters of Blackman High School in Murfreesboro, Tennessee. I was honored to serve the Blaze Band Boosters in various leadership roles for eight years.

So congratulations! You have the potential to mold, shape, and impact the next generation. As you progress through this book, I hope that you will find many takeaways that will immediately benefit your students, instructors, and parents. Thank you for serving – you are awesome!

PART ONE

THE NEED TO LEAD

ONE

How Did I Get Here!

Imagine this. You're on stage before four hundred students and parents who have become your closest friends over the past few years. Standing in the spotlight, you hear the "2001: A Space Odyssey" theme begin to swell from the concert-grade audio system. The crescendo of the kettledrums and brass is ever so familiar. Your anticipation rises as the drums begin to lay down the signature beat of your favorite opening theme song. As the trumpets blast, a professional Elvis[2] tribute artist[3] (yes, we Elvis fans call them "tribute artists") bursts onto the stage. From his jet-black hair to his white zip up boots, this guy's the real deal. The sequins on his white 1970's thunderbird jumpsuit disperse the spotlight into what seem to be a million points of light throughout the auditorium. He grabs the microphone and breaks into his rendition of "Blue Suede Shoes."[4] You begin to dance alongside as cell phone cameras flash and video rolls. Then, he hands you the mike. Mustering up your best to imitate "The King," you belt out,

Blue, blue, blue suede shoes,
You can do anything but lay off of my blue suede shoes!

Well, by now you know that was me on the stage, and what an amazing surprise! This was my final spring banquet with the Blaze Band Boosters, and the experience answered a question that had lingered on my mind for years. *What would that final banquet be like?* The booster event that would bring to a close eight years of service to the program that I dearly loved. The program that had fostered such tremendous growth in both of my children. Would it be painful and sad to let go? Would I simply be satisfied to close that chapter of my life? Or, would I welcome the opportunity to walk away from the role's responsibility? Fortunately, it was a joyful event like I could have never imagined.

Serving as president for the past three years, I had the opportunity to work with an amazing group of dedicated, enthusiastic volunteers. Together, we had

- Met every need for volunteer labor
- Overachieved our fundraising goals
- Transformed the organization's funding model
- Enhanced the band's reputation in the school and community

That night we celebrated the many accomplishments that had contributed to an exceptional learning experience for our students.

Exclamation Point Moments

In my welcome speech to open the banquet, I shared an illustration from Jon Acuff's book, *Start*.[5] Jon says that in every person's life there will be times when you say five simple words – *how did I get here.* Everyone will say them. The response will be different, though, based on the punctuation. Will you answer with a question mark – *how did I get here?* – describing an average, perhaps disappointing milestone in your life? Or will you answer with an exclamation point – *how did I get here!* – reflecting a genuinely awesome achievement? I challenged our students to pursue and achieve their awesome – to celebrate with many exclamation point moments! What kind of awesome do you want to achieve? What is it that will result in an exclamation point moment for you?

To be honored by Elvis was one of the few, truly exceptional exclamation point moments for me. Come along with me for the journey and I'll show you, *how I got here!*

Photo by Regina Jones

TWO

You've Gotta Love It

People don't buy what you do; they buy why you do it.
And what you do simply proves what you believe.[6]

– *Simon Sinek*

There is one overarching requirement for every booster leader: you've gotta love it. You have got to be passionate about the program your booster organization supports. Totally committed. Sold out. All in. A devoted fan of your sports team, band, or choir.

Notice I did not say that you must be a fan of the *booster organization*. Rather, you must be dedicated to serve the *students* your organization supports. Their achievement must be the driving force behind all of your actions.

Before you can effectively lead your organization and motivate others, you must first clearly define what motivates you. Be honest with yourself. Are you doing this in the students' best interest? If not, you should seriously reconsider accepting a leadership role.

Robert and Chase

During my first year with the Blaze Band Boosters, I chaperoned our spring trip to San Antonio. Being a first year chaperone, I was assigned a group of boys who simply were not the best disciplined. A couple of standouts were Robert and Chase. During the first leg of the bus trip, I observed their short, snappy, and sarcastic communication with adults and other students. I watched as another chaperone quickly snapped back at them, which totally shut down the dialogue. I knew I had to take the first step and treat them with respect before they would even consider engaging in a straightforward, transparent conversation. So I overlooked their initial sarcastic remarks and began to establish an element of trust with each one.

Robert had a fancy truck and every electronic gadget that you could imagine. What he lacked, though, was a healthy relationship with his parents. He was from a broken home. Both of his parents had moved on to other relationships and did not seem to have time for him. Instead, they lavished him with material gifts.

As I got to know Chase, he seemed very familiar. I asked him, "In elementary school, were you ever involved in scouts?" His reply was disheartening. "Mr. Caldwell, I haven't been in any school longer than two years. I have moved back and forth between my parents' households, and they have lived in several different places. I wish that I had been able to be in scouts."

Wow! What burdens for these teenagers to bear. In spite of these burdens, I learned that both boys absolutely loved being in the band. Their musical achievements and the sense of community with other students filled the void created by other areas of their lives.

After establishing trust with these two boys, an amazing thing happened. Throughout the course of the trip, they would go out of their way to find me and tell me about their day and their experiences! I had broken through the sarcastic exterior and had begun to make a difference in their lives. Because of my experience with Robert and Chase, I made a commitment to serve the band program and its students in any capacity where there was a need.

Upon our return home, I was unloading the bus when I felt someone tap me on the shoulder. It was Robert. "Mr. Caldwell, I want to introduce you to my dad. Dad, Mr. Caldwell was my chaperone and we had a great time on our trip." I thought to myself, this is what it's all about. I felt as though Robert knew that I cared.

Benefits When Leaders are Motivated to Serve the Students

When you are fully committed to serve the students in the program, you will realize personal benefits. Here are four:

1. **You will play an active role in your own child's life.** The teenage years pass all too quickly. As you near the end of this season in both of your lives, take the opportunity to be involved and to create memories with your child. This is something you will never regret.

2. **Your child will be respected by his or her peers.** There is an interesting dynamic that goes

along with effective booster leadership. Students within the program will respect your leadership, and will also show respect toward your child. Peer acceptance among teenagers can be a huge boost to their self-esteem.

3. **You will help other students grow and mature.** Many of life's lessons are learned outside the classroom. When you support an extracurricular program, you create the opportunity for students to learn those valuable life lessons.

4. **You will set an example of service for the students.** You may not consider yourself a role model, but rest assured, young eyes are paying close attention to the example you set. While you are busy meeting your program's needs, you will show the students how to lead. In effect, you are paying it forward, setting the model for their future leadership.

Risks When Leaders are not Motivated to Serve the Students

There are certain risks that endanger the program when a leader is not fully committed to serve the students. Here are three:

1. **The leader loses interest.** When a leader loses interest, the program's needs may go unmet or only partially met. This is unfortunate because it is the students who stand to lose the most.

2. **The leader derives self worth from serving.** In this case, the leader's ego is fed by the leadership

position. The leader thrives on being in the spotlight. Decisions shift focus from the students' best interest to the leader's best interest.

3. **The booster organization takes precedence over the students it serves.** In some occasions, the booster organization takes a life of its own. The organization's mission – serving the students – is compromised. Decisions are based upon what is best for the leaders or adults without considering the impact or benefit to the students.

To sum it up, there is really only one overarching requirement for booster leadership: you've gotta love it!

Leadership Essential #1: The booster leader must be committed to serve the students.

THREE

Bet Your Paycheck On It

In chapter two, we discussed the motivation that drives every booster leader – a commitment to serve the students – and we examined the benefits of booster leadership. Our primary focus was on you, the booster leader. Now let's take a broader look at the benefits that booster leadership offers students and instructors.

Benefits that Booster Leadership Offers Students

Teenagers have an innate need for acceptance and belonging. A great deal of their self-esteem comes from their association with a group. We want them to get involved in a good group – an extracurricular program. If they cannot connect with a good group, they'll likely connect with a bad group, or even worse, go into isolation. When teenagers associate with bad groups – or go into isolation – they often end up making poor choices, some having life long consequences.

Here are several benefits that teenagers derive from participating in extracurricular programs. Take a moment to reflect on each one and to realize the significant opportunity you have to impact students' lives.

Participating in extracurricular activities helps students
- Encourage others, celebrate wins, and learn from losses

- Develop discipline and establish a solid work ethic
- Learn to set and achieve short-term and long-term goals
- Manage time and prioritize tasks
- Learn the importance of honoring commitments
- Challenge themselves to excel in their activity
- Enjoy better health (physical activity creates more energy, less stress, and a better mood)
- Increase self esteem
- Interact with and learn from other teens with common interests
- Interact with and learn from adults
- Develop and maintain friendships
- Create a lifetime of memories
- Develop a well-rounded foundation of experiences and skills that are sought after by colleges and employers
- Participate in activities that may influence their future careers
- Approach future endeavors with passion

In San Antonio, I saw the benefits that band membership brought Robert and Chase (see chapter two). As a booster leader, you'll also see these benefits demonstrated in your students' lives.

Benefits that Booster Leadership Offers Instructors

Responsibility for students' growth and development may be equally split between educators, students, and parents. Let's look at how they impact student success.

Educators

- School boards and administrators provide challenging, well-rounded curriculums and provide the infrastructure to facilitate learning.
- Teachers instruct, coach, and encourage students along the path of learning.

Students

- Students actively participate in classroom activities and give their best effort.
- Students take ownership in their educational experience and explore options in extracurricular fields of study as they prepare for life.

Parents

- Individually, parents provide the resources needed for their children's learning, partner with teachers, and hold their children accountable to complete their work on time.
- Collectively through booster organizations, parents provide resources needed for extracurricular activities.

There is a disturbing trend in education today. Legislation implemented over the past decade has disproportionately shifted responsibility for student performance toward educators. There are two specific areas that should concern every parent and booster leader – a narrow academic focus and unreasonable instructor accountability.

A Narrow Focus

Current legislation is narrowly focused around two core subjects: English and math. School systems receive federal funding based on their overall student performance on standardized tests in these two subjects. As you may imagine, school systems are motivated to follow the funding, and that puts electives and extracurriculars at risk.

A recent Center on Education Policy[7] study of school districts across the United States found that 62% had *increased* instruction time for English and math. But that increase came at a price. 44% of the districts had actually *decreased* instruction time from one or more other subjects or electives. While we all agree with the need for success in English and math, there has to be a balance between academics and extracurriculars to produce well-rounded graduates. This study reflects the increasing need for booster organizations to support extracurricular activities.

Unreasonable Instructor Accountability

Perhaps even more disturbing than the narrow academic focus are the unreasonable expectations that some school systems place on instructors. In many states, teachers' performance appraisals – and salaries – are linked to their students' test results. I, for one, feel that educators are not exclusively responsible for our students' success.

From our model above, we see that students and parents have an equivalent responsibility.

Parents, it is time that we accept our responsibility for our children's academic success. Are we willing to step up, or are we so self absorbed pursuing our own aspirations that we do not make time to meet our children's needs? Do we have our priorities in order? Do we invest as many hours in the lives of our children as we do in social media and television?

Teachers' salaries are influenced by their students' standardized test scores. What about us? Are we willing to "bet our paycheck on it?" Are we ready to support our children to the extent that we would link a portion of our salaries – our financial livelihood – to our children's test scores?

In this chapter, we've seen the numerous benefits that extracurricular activities offer our students. We've also seen the disturbing trends in education today, which reinforce the need for booster leadership. This is our time to step up, join hands with our instructors, and "bet our paycheck on it! "

Leadership Essential #2: Lead with devotion as if your financial livelihood depends on it.

FOUR

Five Things Most People Will Never Know About Booster Organizations

We've spent the past two chapters examining the case for booster leadership. Now that you know the "why" behind booster organizations – to serve the students and to join hands with instructors for exceptional extracurricular opportunities – let's take a look at "what" they do.

Booster organizations fill four basic roles:

1. **They provide volunteer labor.** Maintaining uniforms and equipment, fundraising, and traveling is labor intensive. There just aren't enough coaches, teachers, and staff members to fill these needs, and they shouldn't have to. Their expertise should be applied to coaching, leading, and instructing the students. Parent volunteers can fill the gaps. When recruiting volunteers, matching the right person to the right role is just as important as filling the role itself.

2. **They support the instructors.** These dedicated professionals pour themselves into our children's lives every day. Many of them serve selflessly, answering a higher calling to inspire students and change lives. But who encourages our teachers? Who inspires them? We must replenish them to overflowing so they can continue to motivate and train our students.

3. **They provide funding for the program.** *Whoa, wait a minute!* you may be thinking. *Shouldn't funding be at the top of the list?* Not necessarily. While funding is the most tangible sign of support for a program, you'll never be able to achieve your funding goals without engaged and motivated volunteers and instructors.

    We know that school board budgets are stretched just to cover the basic necessities of learning. There is simply not enough taxpayer funding to operate all of the extracurricular programs within the school system. And, as a taxpayer, I'm okay with that. Consider the options – pay higher taxes all your life to fund extracurricular programs, or actively contribute and fundraise while you have a child in the program. That's an easy decision for me.

4. **They promote the program within the school and community.** Nothing instills confidence better than community and fan support. Their support contributes to greater teamwork and success. For the student, being a member of a respected program can contribute to higher self-esteem.

Who Can Be a Booster?

It's no surprise that parents and guardians of students in an extracurricular program make up a booster organization's primary membership. But did you know the program's alumni may also join? Alumni make great booster members because they bring spirit and pride they developed as students in the program. You may also extend membership to interested community members.

Booster leadership roles – officers and committee chairs – should be filled by current parents. Parents with children in the program have a vested interest in its success. They need to step up and fill these roles rather than stand by while others take the lead. When you fill leadership roles with others, you deny current parents the opportunity to serve.

By virtue of having a child in the program, parents are always considered booster members, although you'll rarely see some of them. When I was the president of the Blaze Band Boosters, we honored students and their parents with a small gift on Senior Night, the last home football game of the season. It never ceased to amaze me how many parents I had never seen until that night. For whatever reason, they had chosen to spend the past four years in the shadows. This prompted me to think of the things they will likely never know about the organization.

Five Things Most People Will Never Know About Booster Organizations

1. **Booster organizations should incorporate.** The thought that a booster organization is a business entity may never cross your mind. After all, the organization's mission is to support the extracurricular program, not to generate a profit. However, a booster organization conducts normal business transactions, like buying equipment and supplies. Incorporation allows the organization to be

treated as an independent legal entity. Incorporation also protects booster leaders and members from personal liability in the organization's business transactions.

2. **Booster organizations fall under the jurisdiction of the IRS.** The Internal Revenue Service established code 501(c)(3) to exempt certain nonprofit organizations from paying federal income tax. Booster organizations generally qualify for 501(c)(3) status. The IRS has very clear expectations for the operation of these nonprofit organizations, and has been known to audit and levy fines for infractions to the rules.

3. **Nonprofits must file tax returns.** At first this seems counter intuitive. The purpose of the 501(c)(3) is to provide an exemption from paying federal income tax, right? Well, the IRS requires nonprofits to file an informational return. Here's what is required in the return:

   • A written statement of the organization's mission
   • The number of voting members in the governing body
   • The number of individuals employed by the organization
   • The number of volunteers
   • Revenue and expenses
   • Total assets and liabilities

If an organization goes three years without filing a return, its 501(c)(3) status is automatically revoked.

Until reinstated, the organization is not exempt from federal income tax.

4. **School boards provide little, if any, funding for extracurricular activities.** Here's an example. The annual budget to operate an instrumental music program in my county typically starts at $70,000. The school board allocates $5,000 in funding to each high school's program. There are stipulations though – funding must be spent on instructional material for the students. It may not be used to cover expenses such as travel, uniform maintenance, or even equipment maintenance. To put it in perspective, these funds would not cover the replacement cost of a tuba. Don't take it that I'm ungrateful for the school board's funding – it's not that at all. Rather, this example reinforces the need for booster organizations to step up and fill the financial gap, which in this case starts at $65,000.

5. **A booster organization cannot deny participation in an activity, even if a student does not fundraise.** This is another of those topics that seems counter intuitive. If you are going to participate in an activity, doesn't it seem fair that you should help out with fundraising? Well, not in the eyes of the IRS. The essence of the 501(c)(3) is that funds must be distributed equally to all students in the program. This means that the students bringing zero funds into the organization receive the same benefit as the top participants.

Before we move on, let me remind you that I am speaking in laymen's terms from my practical experience. I am neither an attorney nor an accountant. If your organization needs financial advice or other expert assistance, seek the services of a competent professional. While leading my booster organization, there were times when I sought the advice of both an attorney and an accountant. By doing so, I was reassured that we were operating in good faith according to the guidance of the IRS and school board, and with financial integrity.

Circling back, there are two common threads running through this chapter: taking care of people and taking care of money. The booster leader touches many people: parents, volunteers, instructors, alumni, and community members. Positive and motivating interaction with these groups is vital to a thriving booster organization.

The booster leader is accountable for taking care of money. There are many guidelines imposed by the IRS, school boards, and the financial community. Taking care of people and money doesn't have to be hard, it just requires intentional leadership. We'll get into that next.

Leadership Essential #3: The booster leader takes care of people and money.

PART TWO

THE EXECUTIVE
LEADER

FIVE

Lead with Intention

If your actions inspire others to dream more, learn more, do more and become more, you are a leader.

– John Quincy Adams

Think of all of the volunteers in your booster organization, from the president down to the person who serves Gatorade after practice. Do you see them all as leaders? It may be easy to see your president and officers as leaders. After all, they've been elected to lead. But what about your other volunteers – the ones who don't manage activities or make decisions? Do you consider them leaders? John Quincy Adams challenges us to think beyond conventional boundaries and recognize everyone's potential to inspire and lead others.

This book is about leadership – booster leadership. Sure, we'll delve into the specifics that make an organization thrive, but you'll see leadership as the common theme. Regardless of your role in the organization, I will show you how to realize your full leadership potential.

An effective leader leads with intention. The dictionary tells us that intention is "a purpose or goal."[8] Leadership is "to act as a guide" or "to show the way."[9] Therefore, we can say that *intentional leadership is guiding others toward a common purpose.*

The Executive Leader

This part of the book is devoted to the executive leaders – the president and vice president – in a booster organization. They oversee the organization's operations and are accountable for its actions. The booster president typically

- Presides over all meetings
- Oversees all aspects of the organization
- Appoints committees
- Chairs the executive team
- Enforces the organization's bylaws
- Resolves problems in the membership
- Regularly reviews the organization's finances with the treasurer
- Schedules an annual or special audit of records

While all of these tasks are necessary, what really sets an exceptional president apart from the rest? What skills are required to inspire and lead the organization toward a common purpose? Here are five attributes of an effective executive leader:

1. **Passion.** Robert Steven Kaplan says, "Passion is the rocket fuel that helps you perform at your best... It is hard to perform at a high level for a sustained period of time without passion for what you are doing."[10] At times, there will be undesirable and unglamorous tasks, bad days, and occasions when you just don't feel like leading. This is when your

passion to serve the students will motivate you to persevere.

During the recession of 2009 (when the government was bailing-out American automakers), a local car dealer told a reporter, "the trouble at 'XYZ Motors' is that no one wakes up every morning with the 'Diamond' brand on their mind." As an executive leader, you must be the one who wakes up every morning with the best interest of your students, program, and organization on your mind. No one else in the organization has this responsibility.

2. **Inspiration.** The executive leader inspires others to serve. When you lead with passion, others will see that you care and will be inspired to volunteer. It is vitally important to maintain a positive attitude because you set the tone for the entire organization.

3. **Servant leadership.** Effective executive leaders lead by example. If you expect your parents to spend a certain number of hours fundraising (working a concession stand, etc.), then you should be one of the first to work your hours as well. There should be no "executive privileges" for the executive leader.

   Think about it this way; the students in your program are expected to perform with a competitive attitude. Whether on the field or in the performance hall, they are driven to give their all. Shouldn't we serve with the same level of intensity we expect from our students? Lead by example, and walk the talk.

4. **Transparency.** In order to build trust with your volunteers, you must operate transparently. Say what you'll do and do what you say. If you make a

mistake, admit it and move on. Communicate openly, and keep calm if things aren't going your way. Transparent interactions reveal your true character and show others that you care.

5. **Influence.** When you begin to demonstrate the first four attributes, you will build credibility with your volunteers. As people begin to respect your leadership, they will be compelled to follow your vision for the future. In a volunteer setting, their respect for your leadership will give you the relationship power necessary to run the organization.

The Vice President's Role

The vice president's role is often ambiguous and commonly misunderstood. The booster vice president typically

- Presides at meetings in the president's absence
- Performs administrative functions delegated by the president
- Performs other specific duties as outlined in the organization's bylaws

Now, vice presidents, are you ready to go to work? You know exactly what to do, right? Well, maybe not.

Thriving booster organizations prepare their vice presidents to become future presidents. During their tenure, vice presidents learn the responsibilities and expectations of the organization's senior leadership role. They see first hand the issues that face the president, and learn the rationale for addressing those issues. This on-the-job training helps to ensure continuity in leadership year after year.

While preparing for the role of president, the vice president usually takes on a special leadership assignment. Here are four suggestions:

1. **Chair a major fundraising committee.** If your organization relies on one fundraising event for the majority of the program's funding, it is a good idea for an elected officer to oversee it. This will give the executive team greater visibility to the activity and allow them to quickly allocate resources when needed.

2. **Oversee a special project.** Occasionally throughout the life of a program, capital equipment will have to be replaced. Recently, a local high school was faced with the replacement of an aging wrestling mat. This capital expense exceeded their booster organization's annual operating budget, so they established a capital campaign to replace the mat. The vice president organized and oversaw the capital campaign for the mat.

3. **Represent the program within the community.** The vice president makes a great a public relations officer. He can connect with local media outlets to highlight the program's achievements and contributions within the community.

4. **Serve as compliance officer.** Booster organizations must adhere to stringent legal and school board requirements. The vice president is well suited to evaluate the organization's operating

policies and procedures and ensure that all requirements are met.

While serving as vice president of the Blaze Band Boosters, I oversaw the implementation of a new directive from the state board of education.[11] Under the new – and still current – policy, schools may request but not require payment of student fees. Included are "fees for activities and supplies required to participate in all courses offered for credit or grade, including interscholastic athletics and marching band if taken for credit." Furthermore, student grades may not be withheld for these debts.

Working with the band directors, we first decoupled the extracurricular football band program from the daily in-class concert band. This gave students the option to participate in concert band without participating in the extracurricular football band. Then I estimated the directive's impact to income, and recommended changes to future years' budgets. As an officer, I addressed this issue with proper authority and kept the executive team aware of my progress along the way. Meanwhile, the other officers were able to focus on the organization's day-to-day operations.

How Much Time Should I Allocate to Lead my Organization?

Every potential volunteer wants to know how much time the commitment will require. This may be estimated very easily for some roles. For example, let's consider the time requirement for a concessions fundraising chair.

Recruiting volunteers	A hours
Purchasing supplies	+ B hours
Working in the concessions booth	+ C hours
Total hours for one event	X hours

Now, multiply the hours for one event by the total number of events per year.

Total hours for one event	X hours
Total events per year	x Y events
Grand TOTAL hours required by the role	Z hours

It is not that easy to estimate the time required of the executive leader. While I would like to give you a specific number, each organization is different, and a lot depends on your own personal leadership style. Here are some considerations when allocating your time to an executive leadership role:

1. **Balance your time.** Remember to set aside time for your family. Your children are the reason that you volunteered. Don't minimize or squander those teenage years – they pass too fast. And remember to spend time with your spouse – that's who you'll have when the kids have moved on and your booster leadership days are over.

2. **Delegate and allow others to serve.** As an executive leader, you may feel an obligation to be

involved in all of the organization's events and activities. You may feel the need to be there and make sure things are done right, or to simply set a good example for others. And, while you should set a good example for others to follow, you must balance your time and allow others to serve.

When my son crossed over from Cub Scouts to Boy Scouts, we visited several troops to find the right fit for him. On one of our troop visits, the Scoutmaster was away. There was no one in his absence that could fully answer our questions. People would reply, "John takes care of this," or "John takes care of that. John is the hardest working person I know. He sends us email around the clock. I just don't know what we'd do without John." Well, that's the sad truth – they did not know what to do without John. John had minimized his troop's effectiveness by being in the middle of everything. Perhaps unintentionally, he had also taken away the opportunity for others to serve. When volunteers feel that they are not needed, they will fall away from the organization.

3. **No one else will do your role.** If you spread yourself thin participating every time the door is open, you may not have time to properly take care of your leadership duties. Many other people can help meet the needs for volunteer labor. However, no one else is tasked with the organization's overall leadership. First and foremost, your parents, instructors, and students look to you to lead. Don't

let them down by spending your leadership time on tasks that are better suited for others.

Customers and Stakeholders

The executive leader is accountable to the organization's customers and stakeholders. It is important to understand who is included in each of these groups. Customers are the people who your organization touches or benefits. The executive leader's customers are students, parents and guardians, officers, committee chairs, and instructors. You should always strive to benefit your organization's customers.

Stakeholders are the parties that have an influence on your organization, but do not directly benefit from the function of the organization. The executive leader's stakeholders are the IRS, the local school board, the principal and school administrators, and fundraising partners. A booster organization must consider its impact on the stakeholders, and comply with their rules and guidelines.

We have covered a lot of ground in this chapter. We have defined the roles of the president and vice president, and examined five attributes of effective leadership: passion, inspiration, servant leadership, transparency, and influence. When considering how to allocate time, the effective executive leader balances time with family, delegates and allows other to serve, and realizes that no one else in the organization is tasked with its overall leadership. Finally, the executive leader knows her customers and stakeholders, and works to meet their needs.

Leadership Essential #4: Five attributes of the executive leader are passion, inspiration, servant leadership, transparency, and influence.

Leadership Essential #5: The executive leader delegates and allows others to serve.

SIX

Recruit in the Zone

Perhaps the most important task of the executive leader is to match the right volunteer to the right leadership role. In his book, *Good to Great*,[12] Jim Collins compares this process to loading a bus. The leader must not only get the *right people* on the bus, but must get them in the *right seats* on the bus. This is such an important task that it must be done even before the leader decides where to drive the bus.

To recruit the right people into the right roles, you must first recognize their passion and their strengths. Then, assign them to roles where their passion intersects their strengths. I call this recruiting in the zone.

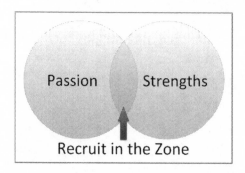

Recognizing a person's passion is not that difficult. Parents want the very best for their children, and are often passionate about their extracurricular programs.

Recognizing a person's strengths requires a little more work. You must build relationships with your parents and learn about their careers, skills, and interests. Once you have established these relationships, you can begin the recruiting process. You'll be able to recruit the salesman to chair the Fundraising Committee, the seamstress to maintain the uniforms, and the web designer to oversee your website.

Here are some best practices that I have learned about recruiting leaders through the years:

1. **Always ask permission.** Whether you are nominating a person for an elected position or selecting someone for an appointed role, always ask the person's permission. This common courtesy will allow you to discuss the requirements of the role and answer questions they may have. Many people will consider it an honor to be asked to serve.

2. **NEVER pressure people into leadership roles.** Don't be a travel agent for guilt trips. Some people have trouble saying no to a hard sell. They may reluctantly accept the role, but later not follow through because their heart was never in it.

3. **Outline the time commitment.** Whenever possible, offer a realistic assessment of the role's time commitment. Some people are willing to accept a year-round role, while others prefer a short-term assignment. By clearly defining the role's time commitment, you may alleviate potential volunteer burn out.

4. **As a rule of thumb, assign one person to only one leadership role.** When you assign a volunteer

to only one role, you set her up for success. She'll be able to focus all of her energy in that one area. You'll also benefit by having a broad number of volunteers engaged in the organization.

5. **Recruit prior trip chaperones.** Most booster organizations sponsor their program's travel. Trip chaperones make perfect recruits for future leadership roles. They fund their own travel, and in many cases use their vacation days for the trip. While traveling, they meet and interact with the students, and develop an affinity for the program.

6. **Fill all leadership roles before the annual kick-off meeting.** Always start a new year with a full leadership staff. The beginning of the year is the perfect time for committee chairs to recruit volunteers. Do not miss the opportunity to engage new families and parents by failing to have committee leadership in place.

7. **Understand there is no guarantee of success when recruiting volunteer leaders.** Just because you follow these best practices, you are not always guaranteed success. One of our most profitable fundraisers was working concessions for a local university during football season. In selecting a chair for this important committee, I looked first to the most active volunteers from the prior year. Erik was experienced in running the concession stand, from food preparation to customer service.

Erik and I spoke at length about the time commitment and the fundraiser's importance to our booster organization. After a week's consideration he replied, "I realize the time commitment is long, but I also realize how important this fundraiser is to the booster organization. I will arrange my schedule so that I can chair this committee."

Wow, I thought, *he has really made an informed and thoughtful decision.* I was confident that the committee was in good hands, but it didn't take long for that to change!

Erik emailed me after the university's first football game. He explained that he had underestimated the role's requirements, and that he would not be able to chair the committee for the remainder of the season. So I went back to the drawing board, and was fortunate to identify a competent and dedicated replacement.

Even after taking the necessary steps to place the right people in the right leadership roles, there is still an element of risk when working with volunteers. Don't be discouraged, though. In my tenure as president of the Blaze Band Boosters, I filled more than sixty roles. Erik was only one of two recruits who pulled out and did not fulfill his commitment. In chapter twenty-nine, Empower Committees to Succeed, we'll take a look at a high functioning committee, starting with the recruiting process that identified its leader.

Leadership Essential #6: Recruit in the zone where a person's passion intersects his or her strengths.

SEVEN

Motivate with an Attitude of Gratitude

People often say that motivation doesn't last. Well,
neither does bathing – that's why we recommend it daily.

– Zig Ziglar

As the executive leader, you set the tone for the organization, and that starts by motivating the parents. In order to fill the many needs for volunteer labor, you have to create contagious energy that draws in people to serve. You can't expect others to get excited about the program if you don't show that excitement yourself. A fellow booster president once told me that he considers himself the biggest "cheerleader" for his program.

Here are a few effective ways to motivate your parents to serve:

1. **Create a culture of acceptance.** Always welcome and encourage someone new to get involved. We know that it can be awkward for new students transitioning into the program, and it can be just as awkward for their parents. When incoming parents see a vibrant group of volunteers, they may also be compelled to volunteer.

2. **Encourage participation, and avoid the hard sell.** Help people see where they best fit. I was once

involved in a scout troop where the adult leaders met with incoming parents and laid down very stringent expectations for participation. Everyone was expected to participate, but people weren't assigned to roles according to their strengths. The result? Many people were unprepared for the roles in which they were placed. This was awkward and stressful for the misplaced parents, and was not productive for the troop.

3. **Bring the conversation home.** The high school years draw to a close the season of life where your children are at home. They will soon be off to college and into careers. Encourage your parents to take advantage of this opportunity to be involved in their children's lives.

4. **Express the need and share the progress.** Clearly define the need for volunteer labor and explain that the school board does not provide it. Many people will be motivated to step in and help simply by knowing the need exists. And when they volunteer, share with them the progress toward meeting the organization's goals. People want to know that they are helping to make a difference.

5. **Recognize their service and express gratitude.** Recognition and gratitude are perhaps the greatest sources of motivation available to you. Likewise, the absence of recognition and gratitude is one of the greatest demotivators in an organization.

The executive leader must strive to ingrain recognition and gratitude into the organization's culture. There are three types of recognition that are essential to a thriving booster organization:

1. **Individual recognition.** A handshake and heartfelt "thank you" will go a long way. Most people don't expect anything in return for their volunteer labor – they just want to be appreciated. Individual recognition should be timely, generally during or immediately after the event they served.

2. **Written recognition.** Written recognition should go along with, but not take the place of, individual recognition. Written recognition may be in the form of a handwritten note, or it may be delivered electronically by email, text, or voice mail. At the close of a major event, always provide written recognition to the volunteers. Written recognition means the most when it comes from the booster president or instructor.

3. **Public recognition.** Every organization has volunteers who continually give of their time. Take the initiative to recognize them publicly during a booster meeting, year-end banquet, or other appropriate forum.

While serving as president of the Blaze Band Boosters, we saw the need to create an award to honor volunteers who went above and beyond the call of duty in service to the organization. Here's how we got started.

One year, our season opening football game was about sixty-five miles from home. We had suffered August's triple digit heat for several days in a row. One of our parents pulled the band's flatbed trailer with his own vehicle. Although we thought the trailer was roadworthy, the tire pressure had become low over the summer. As a result, one of the under inflated tires overheated and blew out on the return trip home. It not only blew out, it disintegrated into shreds. And, as our luck would have it, we didn't have a spare. Another parent helped rescue the crippled trailer, and it was well after 1:00 AM before they returned all of our equipment safely to the band room.

This prompted us to create the Blaze Band Shout Out, an award to honor volunteers like these parents who had gone above and beyond in the call of duty. Over the course of three years, we awarded more than fifty Shout Outs to volunteers from both inside and outside our organization.

BLAZE BAND SHOUT OUT

Kenneth & Tracy Black
Presented to

The safe navigation and recovery of the flatbed trailer after a tire blowout on Interstate 24, August 20, 2010.

Thank you for your support of the Blaze Band!!!

Brenda Monson

September 14, 2010
Date

Brad Franklin

While it is vitally important to recognize the work of your volunteers, there are three common pitfalls to avoid:

1. **Failing to recognize everyone who helped.** This is an area where some leaders unintentionally fail. Be diligent to include all volunteers when giving recognition.

2. **Being late with recognition.** When recognizing volunteers for their service, time is of the essence. With individual and written recognition, you have a very short window of opportunity. Don't let that opportunity pass without expressing your gratitude.

3. **Failing to be specific with your praise.** Don't be generic when it comes to recognition. People love to hear how their efforts have helped the organization reach a goal.

An effective executive leader sets the tone for the organization and motivates others to serve. One of the greatest motivational tools for the executive leader is recognition. When you offer heartfelt, specific, and timely praise to everyone who serves, people will want to continually volunteer.

Leadership Essential #7: Recognition is the greatest motivator available to the executive leader.

EIGHT

Create a Unified Team

Thriving booster organizations function as a unified team. There is nothing as distracting, disruptive, and potentially devastating as factions or cliques that may split away from the organization and go their own direction. When this occurs, the focus is taken off the program and the students stand to lose the most.

The executive leader must take proactive measures to promote and maintain unity. In my experience, there are at least six ways to promote unity within a booster organization:

1. **Lead.** This may seem very simple and obvious, but it is important for the executive leader to provide clear direction for the organization. Do not create a situation where others have to fill the gap. People look to you for direction, and they must feel as if the program's needs, as well as their own needs, are being met.

2. **Communicate.** It's not enough to simply create your plan; you must make sure everyone knows your plan. Share your direction and goals with the parents in your organization. Ensure their buy-in to help achieve those goals. Do not leave anything to speculation, which may create the perception of a lack of leadership.

3. **Be transparent.** Even if the news is bad, let everyone know the situation. Here's an example to describe the importance of transparency.

At the start of a school year, our county school board issued the directive that booster organizations with individual student accounts were to immediately consolidate them into one general fund for the organization. At the time, individual student accounts were a part of our funding model, and our families would collectively "lose" $19,000 if we immediately consolidated. Families had accrued these funds toward future year's fees, the spring trip, instruments, lessons, and supplies. As you may imagine, this news sent major shock waves throughout our organization. Our parents wanted to know if they were going to lose funds that they had accrued in good faith to support their students' music education.

While I clearly understood that consolidation was the right thing to do (more on this in chapter fifteen), I held a heartfelt obligation to our parents. I set out to establish a transition plan that would allow our families to manage their funds as we consolidated accounts. Over a six-week period, I communicated the status of this initiative to our parents. Many times, I didn't have the answers, but I did communicate the steps we were taking with the school board, our principal, an attorney, and our accountant. Fortunately, we were able to arrive at a resolution that prevented students' funds from being immediately swept away into a general fund.

Communicating transparently with our parents maintained unity throughout this tumultuous time. More than once, parents told me that they would have taken their complaints directly to the school board had they not understood my plan and seen my progress. Instead, our unified approach helped us to be part of the solution in accomplishing the school board's directive.

4. **Create a culture of acceptance.** As we saw in chapter seven, creating a culture of acceptance motivates others to get involved. It also promotes unity and inclusion. Be intentional in accepting people into the organization. If you don't, they may seek out others who also feel outcast and create a clique.

5. **Let people know that they are valued.** This is another theme repeated from chapter seven, and it is so important to your organization's well being. Recognize your volunteers and let them know they are needed to accomplish the organization's goals and to help the extracurricular program succeed. Nothing turns people off faster than feeling like their service is not valued.

6. **Address negative issues in a timely manner when they arise.** Because booster organizations are made up of volunteers, and volunteers are human, misunderstandings and issues will arise. Notice that I didn't say that issues *may* arise, I said they *will* arise. And when issues arise, the executive leader must address them before they are allowed to infect the organization. To quote the famous law

enforcement officer, Barney Fife, you've got to "Nip it! Nip it in the bud!"[13] Unaddressed issues will fester and lead to gossip, the taking of sides, and division within the organization.

While recruiting committee chairs, Laverne told me that she did not want to continue leading the Band Camp Committee during her daughter's upcoming senior year. She offered her support to Janet, the newly recruited committee chair, for what should have been a smooth transition. However, as Janet began planning for the upcoming camp, Laverne became very difficult to get along with. She exerted her influence and demanded that Janet do things exactly as they had always been done. She dismissed Janet's ideas for improvement and, even worse, told Janet her ideas were going to fail. Later, Laverne denied stepping down from her leadership position, and told Janet to step aside and serve as an assistant!

This situation required executive leadership intervention! I first confronted Laverne, and reminded her that she had given up her leadership role. Furthermore, I explained that she would not be allowed to treat other volunteers in this manner. Then, I reassured Janet that she was the leader and had the full support of the executive leadership team. Laverne reluctantly stepped aside, and Janet went on to flourish in her role. She implemented many improvements that helped the students excel in band camp.

In summary, the executive leader unites the organization by leading and communicating with transparency, creating a culture of acceptance, valuing people, and addressing issues as they arise.

Leadership Essential #8: Unity must be a priority and is accomplished through intentional leadership.

NINE

Prepare to Thrive Throughout the Year

By failing to prepare, you are preparing to fail.

– Benjamin Franklin

In chapters five through eight, we examined the "soft skills" of executive leadership. Those are the skills that help you build meaningful relationships and influence others. Now it's time to focus on the tactical, or operational, skills necessary in running a successful and thriving booster organization. We'll kick things off in this chapter with the executive leader's annual calendar of events.

The first thing the executive leader should do to begin a new year is to develop an annual calendar. The time spent here will pay huge dividends throughout the course of the year. An established calendar will help you maintain focus on current events, anticipate upcoming events, and accomplish your organization's goals.

Let's get started. Begin with a blank calendar representing the fiscal year of your organization. For example, my organization's fiscal year ran from June 1st through May 31st. Follow these steps to develop your calendar:

1. **Write in important dates from the school calendar.** These will include semester start and

end dates, holidays, and breaks. I found it helpful to include half days – days when students are dismissed early for teacher development and workshops.

2. **Enter dates for the major events that draw the majority of parents.** There are surprisingly very few opportunities for you to speak to the majority of your parents in one sitting. Throughout the year, there may only be three or four major events that draw in most parents. You should anticipate these events and craft your messages to capitalize on the opportunity to address the broad audience. These were my major events and the themes for the messages I delivered:

- **Annual kick-off meeting in May.** The "grand tour" introduction to the organization for incoming parents and students.
- **Band camp cookout (final evening of band camp week).** What to expect through the upcoming quarter (fundraising, volunteer labor needs, etc.).
- **Spring trip readiness meeting.** Expectations for travelers; annual performance to budget (in preparation for future year budgeting).
- **Spring banquet.** Reflection on the year's achievements, congratulations to graduating seniors, inspiration for returning students.

Notice that these events are not games or performances – those are for the students to show their progress and skill. Also these are not routine booster meetings, which are typically attended by only the "core group" of volunteers.

3. **Add dates of games and performances.** This will give you advance visibility to nonstandard dates and locations. For example, booster organizations serving football teams, bands, cheerleading squads, and dance teams need to know if there are any Thursday evening football games on the schedule. This deviation from a typical Friday evening schedule may require parent volunteers to make special arrangements when working concessions, moving equipment, or helping with other special tasks. Additionally, an away game on any night to a far away school will require special planning for transportation.

4. **Insert fundraising events.** A visual picture of your fundraising schedule will help you assess your manpower needs. It will help you identify conflicts and bottlenecks if you provide labor to work fundraising events. For example, we worked concessions and merchandising stands for two universities and one professional football team. Typically, we'd have multiple fundraising events one or two days each year. Getting these dates on the calendar allowed us to recruit additional labor and fulfill our obligations.

5. **Merge in booster meetings.** Many organizations hold standing booster meetings on a certain evening of each month. Ours was the second Tuesday of the month. Even with a standing meeting schedule, you should look ahead for any interferences with the

school calendar, games, or performances. I experienced interferences around Christmas break, spring break, and the winter band concert. During those months, I would reschedule the booster meeting, usually to the third Tuesday of the month. Whenever you reschedule, be sure to communicate the change, else you may have a few parents to show up on the regularly scheduled evening.

6. **Establish newsletter publication & distribution dates.** Many organizations publish a monthly newsletter. Months roll by quickly for parent volunteers, and it is easy to let publication dates slip if you are not intentional in scheduling. We posted the Blaze Band newsletter to our website, Tweeted a link, and mailed a hard copy to our families. My goal was for hard copies to arrive in homes on Friday or Saturday prior to our Tuesday booster meetings. To accomplish this, I established a series of deadlines. The first deadline was for committee chairs and band directors to submit their content. The next was for completion of the newsletter. The final deadline was for distribution and mailing of hard copies.

You will find the newsletter publication calendar to be one of your most useful tools. At the beginning of the year, distribute this calendar to your secretary, committee chairs, instructor, webmaster, and office volunteers. This will let them know what to expect throughout the year, and they'll be able to book these important dates on their personal calendars. You'll still want to remind them of upcoming dates each month, but they will appreciate the advance notice.

7. **Schedule special activities or services that have not already been captured.** As you work through the scheduling process, be sure to add any other important activity or service that your organization offers to your program. For example, you may arrange a letterman jacket sale for your students. Schedule preliminary meetings with your vendor, and then establish dates for the sale. Letterman jackets make great Christmas presents, so remember to allocate delivery time.

If you have your end-of-year banquet off campus, add a reminder to your calendar to book the off-site venue. Facilities that offer comfortable seating, provisions to serve a meal, and audio/video capabilities – at an affordable rate – are hard to come by. Make your reservation early, even before your Banquet Committee begins their activities.

Now that you have completed your annual calendar, you have your roadmap for the year. Share the entire calendar with your executive team and committee chairs, and parse out items to individual groups as necessary. The main benefit is that you, the executive leader, have a resource that will guide you throughout the course of the year.

Leadership Essential #9: A comprehensive annual calendar of events provides a roadmap for the executive leader.

TEN

Excel Throughout the Midterm

In many ways, leading a booster organization is like running a small business. With an entrepreneurial spirit, the executive leader casts a vision for the organization's future. From this vision, goals are developed for the midterm.

Planning for the midterm is vital to a booster organization's sustained success. The process of midterm planning compels you to anticipate longer range needs that may not be evident through the organization's day-to-day operations. By its nature, booster leadership may create a short-term mindset. With volunteers serving one to two year terms, it may be easy for them to assume the attitude to "keep the lights on" until they rotate out.

Let's take a look at the steps to create a midterm plan for your booster organization.

Cast a Vision

Vision is the ability to look beyond today's current condition and see something better in the future. Vision for the future is not something mysterious that comes to you in a dream. Rather, it is intentionally developed by carefully considering many factors that are vital to your organization's health. Here are five considerations when developing your vision:

1. **What is important to the instructor?** What are her dreams for the program? How can the booster organization help make those dreams a reality? What new technology and trends does she see on the horizon for the sport or field of study? How will that impact the program's success in the midterm?

2. **What is necessary to maintain operations?** Evaluate the age and condition of your equipment, uniforms, and facilities. What is the expected life of these assets? How long will it take to raise the funds to repair or replace them?

3. **What are your opportunities for improvement?** Do a little brainstorming. Think big! Imagine what you would do if you weren't bound by money and time. Is there an unmet need that has been written off because of a perceived inability to address it? Is there an opportunity to build the organization's reputation within the community?

4. **What are other programs doing?** What are the very best programs doing? Look beyond your immediate area and evaluate programs at the state and national level. It is easier than you would imagine to benchmark other organizations these days. You can learn so much through an evening of web surfing. Most organizations list their leaders' contact information on their websites. A few emails sent to the right individuals may help you identify ways to take your organization to the "next level."

5. **What ideas do other officers and leaders have?** Remember, they have a vested interest in the

program just like you, and they see many different aspects of the organization. What needs or opportunities do they see from their vantage point?

As you develop your vision for the future, you will find that your ideas fit into one of two categories: internal or external. Internal initiatives impact the organization and the program itself. External initiatives build the organization's "brand" within the school and community. Here are a few examples of each.

Internal Initiatives

- Build a football field house
- Replace a wardrobe of uniforms
- Upgrade a practice field or facility
- Purchase an equipment trailer
- Purchase and install a new scoreboard

External Initiatives

- Conduct a promotional media campaign to:
  - Build your organization's reputation (this is especially appropriate for a new school, program, or organization)
  - Repair the organization's reputation (if the careless acts of your predecessors have left you with a mess to clean up)
- Participate in community outreach projects

Develop Goals

Once you have a vision for the future, it is time to refine that vision into actionable goals. Dave Ramsey says that, "Goals are visions and dreams with work clothes on."[14] Well-defined goals give the executive leader a platform and a call to action to rally the troops.

Here are some best practices when converting your vision into goals for your organization:

1. **Align your goals with your organization's mission.** Just because an idea surfaces through the brainstorming process doesn't mean that it is in the students' best interest. Before you embark upon a multi-year capital campaign, be sure that the initiative is aligned with your organization's mission – to enhance the students' learning experience – rather than an adult leader's pet project. By aligning your goals with your organization's mission, you will be sure to hit the right target.

2. **Select only one or two goals.** It is very difficult for an organization to meet its day-to-day needs and achieve several longer-range goals. I recommend setting only one or two. The authors of *The 4 Disciplines of Execution* share these insightful findings from years studying high performing teams:[15]

   • Teams that focus on two or three goals beyond their day-to-day activities often accomplish them.

   • Teams that set four to ten goals, however, only tend to achieve one or two.

- Teams that set eleven or more goals lose all focus and are unable to accomplish any of their goals.

3. **Set SMART goals.** Well-defined goals are the goals that get achieved. Here's a breakdown of the SMART acronym:

- **Specific.** Clearly state the goal. For example, "purchase an 18' x 7' tandem axle enclosed trailer" is better than "purchase a trailer."

- **Measurable.** Establish a unit of measurement and a target value in order to track your progress toward achieving the goal. For example, "raise $20,000 to purchase a new wrestling mat" is better than "raise money to purchase a new wrestling mat."

- **Achievable.** Goals for the midterm should stretch the organization, but not to the point of discouraging your volunteers. Goals should be within the organization's influence and control to achieve.

- **Realistic.** Just because a school in a large city with generous alumni donors installs artificial turf on their football field doesn't mean that a small school in a rural area will be able to do the same.

- **Time bound.** Goals without time limits fall prey to procrastination. A goal with a deadline is a booster organization's call to action.

Communicate the Goals to Achieve the Vision

When everyone works toward common goals and vision, there is unity within the organization. The executive leader must thoroughly communicate the goals to the organization. In his book, *Visioneering*, Andy Stanley says that a leader has to discuss the vision of the organization twenty-one times before people start to hear it. There are many competing priorities for your volunteers' time, so take advantage of every opportunity to communicate your goals and vision for the organization.

In summary, you should always strive to leave your organization better than you found it. Take a step back and evaluate the organization's needs beyond the urgent here and now. Cast a vision, set goals, and execute them throughout the midterm.

What will be your legacy?

Leadership Essential #10: The prudent leader casts a vision for the future and strives to achieve that vision throughout the midterm.

ELEVEN

Collaborate with the Executive Team

The executive team is the catalyst that propels the booster organization. Collaborating together, they plan and decide upon courses of action to achieve the organization's goals. The executive leader guides the executive team and facilitates their efforts for maximum effectiveness and success. Let's focus on the attributes of a productive executive team.

Executive Team Members

The executive team is obviously comprised of the organization's elected officers. Additionally, there are other members whose participation is vital to the organization's success:

- **The program instructor.** The teacher, coach, or music/arts director is an integral executive team member. The instructor helps align the booster organization's activities with the extracurricular program's needs. Additionally, the instructor provides an interface between the booster organization and school administrators.

The organization's executive team may include more than one instructor. For example, an assistant coach or assistant band director may serve on the executive team along with the head coach or senior band director. However, in order to maintain accountability, many school systems limit the number of instructors who may serve on the executive team. My county's school board has the following policy: "A majority of the voting members of the group's [executive] board may not be school employees (including board members, the Director of Schools, coaches, trainers, or sponsors)."[16]

- **Select committee chairs.** Sometimes it makes sense to include the chairs of significant committees on the executive team. Here are a couple of examples from my experience. In succession planning for the treasurer to rotate out of the organization, we created an ad hoc Finance Committee of one. The intention was for this individual to spend the year learning as much as possible about the treasurer's role in anticipation of filling it the following year. We included the Finance Committee chair on the executive team to accelerate this transition.

At one point, we included the Fundraising Committee chair on the executive team. At the time, we provided labor for concessions and merchandising booths for two local universities and our NFL team. These partnerships provided a majority of the funding coming into the program, and it was important that the executive team had visibility to these operations.

Here's an important note – while the Finance and Fundraising Committee chairs sat on the executive team, they did not have voting privileges. Committee chairs are appointed, and I did not want to create the perception that the elected officers were filling the executive team with appointed members to sway the vote on critical decisions.

Executive Team Meetings

A booster organization's executive team should meet face to face at least once a month. Executive team meetings may correspond with monthly booster meetings. My executive team met forty-five minutes prior to the monthly booster meeting. You will find times when the executive team needs to meet or communicate outside of the routine monthly schedule. Here are a few examples:

1. **Special called meetings to address specific topics.** I found that three additional annual meetings were necessary. The first was in May to prepare for the annual kick-off meeting for all new and returning students. The second meeting was in August to get everyone focused and "on the same page" for the first half year's activities. The third meeting was in January to draft a fundraising plan for the following year.

2. **Impromptu meetings by conference call.** Occasionally, an important decision with an urgent deadline will arise that requires discussion by the executive team. For those who cannot join in person on short notice, remember to take advantage of modern communication technology. Most smartphones have built-in speakers, and many cell phone voice plans include a conference call option. For a short meeting, this technology will facilitate a

quick discussion and allow a decision to be agreed upon.

3. **Email.** Email is one of the most valuable communication tools for the executive team. Within a matter of hours (sometimes minutes), executive team members can evaluate materials, provide comments, and make decisions. When using email, be aware of these challenges:

- **Version control.** When emailing attachments for collaboration by the team, it is sometimes hard to know which version of a file includes the most recent revisions. A cloud-based storage service, like Dropbox,[17] is a great resource to resolve this issue. Rather than having each team member revise the file that he or she received with an email, team members access one common file in the cloud. Cloud-based storage also provides the executive team a repository for materials that may be accessed for reference at a later date.

- **Unclear proposals.** Occasionally, a decision will have to be made that doesn't warrant a special face-to-face meeting, but has a deadline prior to the next regularly scheduled meeting. In this case, it is very important for the executive leader to clearly state the proposal at hand. There should be no question what the executive team is being asked to approve. Cost, time, and other critical details must be clearly stated. Here's an example proposal for approval:

The Merchandising Committee chair may purchase 200 orange t-shirts at a cost of $5 each, with a one time set-up fee of $50. Shirts to be screen printed with the attached logo XYZ. Total expenditure is not to exceed $1050. Shirts to be purchased no later than September 20th.

The Executive Leader's Responsibilities

As stated above, the executive leader guides the executive team and facilitates their discussion. Here are six steps to ensure the team's success:

1. **Distribute detailed agendas.** No less than two days prior to the meeting, send a draft agenda to the executive team and solicit their input for meeting topics. Incorporating their feedback, issue a final agenda no less than one day prior to the meeting. Be sure to include all supporting material for the team to review prior to the meeting.

2. **Establish ground rules.** With a new administration, set ground rules for executive team meetings. Solicit the team's input, and obtain their buy-in. Here are a few thought starters: be on time, have only one conversation at a time, listen actively, participate actively, maintain focus on the topic, treat others with respect, and apply "Vegas rules" – what's said in the room stays in the room. These rules of engagement, once understood and accepted by all, will help set a collaborative atmosphere for meetings throughout the year.

3. **Establish the process for decision making.** I prefer that the executive team make decisions by consensus. We'll discuss that more in the next chapter.

4. **Preside over the meetings.** Executive leaders, this is your role. Don't default this responsibility to the instructor. He has plenty to do running the extracurricular program. Also, remember the purpose for the booster organization is to garner parent involvement, so don't let an instructor with a strong personality take over.

   When presiding over meetings, keep the discussion focused on the topic at hand and do not stray off on tangents. These unintended tangents can hijack a meeting and keep you from getting through your agenda.

5. **Clearly state decisions and assignments.** Decisions should be clearly stated (like our example proposal above), and assignments should be made with the same clarity. Be sure that every assignment has a realistic deadline. Recap decisions and assignments before you adjourn so that each team member will leave with a clear understanding.

6. **Document the outcome of the meeting.** The secretary should issue meeting minutes within 24 hours to reinforce decisions and assignments.

Leadership Essential #11: The executive leader guides the executive team and facilitates their discussion to ensure success.

TWELVE

Foster Decisions by Consensus

*People don't always have to have their way, but they
have to have their say.*

– Kent Vaughn

Chances are your organization's constitution and bylaws require decisions to be made by parliamentary procedure. Robert's Rules of Order, first published in 1876 by Henry M. Robert,[18] are the most commonly referenced rules of parliamentary procedure and define the voting process in explicit detail. These rules can be valuable when administering a vote to a large group like your booster organization because proposals are approved by a majority of members.

However, when decisions are made by majority vote, there are winners and there are losers. The losers have little incentive to support the decision, as their voices have not been heard throughout the decision-making process. As a result, unity within the organization may be compromised and factions may develop. Small groups like your executive team need a decision-making process that values all members' opinions and promotes harmony among the team. I suggest you exchange Robert's 19th century rules for a more collaborative 21st century decision-making method.

Consensus decision making is a group decision-making process that seeks the consent of all participants.[19] By definition, consensus is "a general agreement about something: an idea or opinion that is shared by all the people in a group."[20] Consensus decision making allows all participants to contribute to the discussion. Proposals may be modified in order to address concerns raised by the group. While full agreement is desired, it is not necessary in order to move forward with a decision. What is necessary, however, is that each member agrees to support the group's decision.

Here are three benefits of consensus decision making:

1. **Decisions are more definitive.** Through the group's collaborative efforts, potential concerns are surfaced and may be immediately addressed. As a result, proposals may be modified, allowing for more appropriate decisions to be made.

2. **Implementation is more successful.** Decisions that have been made in a collaborative environment tend to garner a greater level of cooperation in implementation.

3. **Unity within the group is greater.** Consensus decision making fosters greater cohesion within the group because everyone is given the opportunity to voice an opinion and influence the final decision.

The Executive Leader's Role

The executive leader facilitates decision making by the executive team. There are seven steps for successful decision making by consensus:

1. **Clearly define the proposal in question.** Begin the process by specifically stating the proposal, including the parameters of cost and time. You may want to revisit the example proposal in chapter eleven.

2. **Provide background information in advance of the meeting.** Distribute background information along with the meeting agenda. This will allow the executive team to become familiar with the issues before the meeting.

3. **Invite a subject matter expert to speak to the executive team.** It is common for a committee chair to gather information for a potential future purchase. Invite the committee chair to share the business case for the purchase and to answer the executive team's questions.

4. **Collaboratively discuss the proposal.** Encourage the team to engage in a healthy discussion of the proposal's pros and cons. Remind them to abide by the meeting ground rules established at the beginning of the school year (see chapter eleven). When facilitating the discussion, watch for and intervene if

   - **The team gets off on a tangent.** Help the team to regain focus on the original proposal if they get sidetracked. While it is okay to modify the original proposal, don't allow the team to lose valuable time discussing unrelated issues.

   - **A team member does not appear to be participating.** Occasionally, a team member will sit quietly during a discussion. Draw that team member into the discussion by asking his thoughts about the proposal.

- **The team engages in groupthink.** Groupthink is a psychological phenomenon that occurs within a group of people in which the desire for harmony or conformity in the group results in an incorrect or deviant decision-making outcome.[21] In this situation, team members may try to avoid conflict by going along with the group, even if they have reservations and concerns about the proposal. If you see this happening, remind the team of "Vegas rules" (what's said in the room stays in the room). Then take them out of their comfort zone with challenging questions from alternate viewpoints (playing the "Devil's advocate"). Don't be afraid to ask difficult or unpopular questions – that goes along with your leadership role.

5. **Gather additional information if necessary.** While presiding over the Blaze Band Boosters' executive team, we needed an All Terrain Vehicle (ATV) to move our equipment. The Truck & Equipment Committee chair proposed the purchase of an electric ATV to the executive team. Frankly, we were concerned that the electric power train would not meet our needs. We postponed the decision until the following meeting so that we could evaluate a demonstrator model. This gave us the opportunity to confirm that the level of power and the duration of

the electric charge would be sufficient for our application.

6. **Modify the proposal if necessary.** The ability to modify a proposal before it is approved and implemented is one of the greatest benefits of making decisions by consensus. Modifying the proposal may dramatically reduce the potential for failure once the decision is implemented.

7. **Finalize the decision.** This is the most important step of the process. Remember, not everyone has to *agree* with the decision, but they must all *support* it with one voice. Christopher Avery[22] identified six responses you're likely to hear from team members, and the corresponding actions:

   1. **Unqualified yes.** Move forward.
   2. **Perfectly acceptable.** Move forward.
   3. **I can live with the group's decision.** Move forward.
   4. **I trust the group and will not block this decision but need to register my disagreement.** Move forward.
   5. **I feel no sense of unity as a group and think more work is needed before deciding.** Stay put.
   6. **I do not agree and feel the need to stand in the way of adopting this decision.** Stay put.

Once a decision has been made, establish an implementation plan that everyone supports. Include in your plan a person in charge, a budget for expenses, and a deadline for completion.

In summary, traditional majority voting may compromise unity and lead to factions within your organization. Consensus decision making offers a collaborative approach that lends itself well to the executive team. As the executive leader, facilitate consensus decision making for more definitive decisions, more successful implementations, and greater unity within the organization.

Leadership Essential #12: Decisions made by consensus foster unity among the executive team.

THIRTEEN

Conduct Inspiring Meetings

"Hello, my name is Dan Caldwell and it is an honor to serve as your booster president." With these words, I brought booster meetings to life. This was my time to encourage and energize the faithful group of volunteers who made up the Blaze Band Boosters.

As the spokesperson for your organization, conduct meetings with intention and passion. Many parents will only see you leading meetings, and they'll form opinions of the organization based on the example you set. Use this opportunity to win them over and draw them into active membership. These nine steps will help you conduct inspiring and meaningful meetings:

1. **Spark interest with "teaser" advertisements.** Generate interest by advertising a couple of intriguing meeting topics in advance. Always look for a "hook" that will draw people to the meeting.

2. **Speak with confidence and passion.** The fear of public speaking is universal among people around the world. However, with practice and attention to a few simple details, you can take charge of that fear. Here are a few pointers to help you improve your public speaking skills:

   • **Introduce yourself.** Don't assume that everyone knows who you are. Open every meeting with an introduction, using the opportunity to show support and enthusiasm for the program.

- **Smile.** When you smile, you convey a warm, friendly, approachable demeanor. A smile helps you build trust with your audience. Studies show that when you smile, endorphins are released in your body that reduce stress and generate happiness.
- **Stand up straight.** Good posture expresses confidence and energy. Arch your back, pulling your shoulders back and down. Plant your feet firmly on the ground about shoulder width apart. This will keep you from swaying back and forth. Keep your chin slightly raised to visually communicate that you're in control.
- **Make eye contact.** As you speak, look around the room and make eye contact with individuals in the audience. This will show that you are confident and trustworthy, and that you, yourself, believe in your message. Respect your audience by making eye contact with them.
- **Speak up.** Speak loud enough for everyone to hear you. Clearly pronounce every word. Pace yourself and intentionally pause to allow the audience to absorb your message.
- **Don't distract the audience.** Have you ever missed the point of a speaker's message because you were distracted by his use of filler words? We tend to rely on words such as "ah," "um," and "you know" while we compose our thoughts

in the transition between topics. To prevent this distraction, simply pause between topics.

Poor grammar is another distraction to avoid. The English language is full of grammatical nuances. Although your audience may overlook poor grammar from time to time, make a conscientious effort to use proper grammar and to avoid slang words.

Overusing a single word or phrase is known as a verbal tic. Here's an example. I once worked for a man who overused the word "basically." This became a distraction for those listening to him. His employees even counted the number of times he used the word "basically" during his staff meetings. This verbal tic decreased his effectiveness as a communicator and often undermined his message because he attached a qualifier – "basically" – to his point.

- **Speak with enthusiasm.** Show your passion and excitement for the program! Make others want to volunteer so they can have what you have. But be careful not to overdo it. Your audience will detect when enthusiasm is forced, and they may become uncomfortable.

- **Move away from the lectern.** Engage your audience by moving around the room, paying attention to different people. When answering a question, move closer to the person who asked it. Be careful, however, not to pace back and forth – this will convey that you are nervous.

- **Be yourself.** We have covered a lot of ground with these pointers. In your quest to engage your audience, remember to be yourself. Your audience knows you, and they will know if you are putting on a front. Always be genuine and transparent.

3. **Create a welcoming environment.** Adults are odd creatures at times. We are prone not to introduce ourselves to people sitting right beside us! At the beginning of a meeting, have everyone stand up and meet two people they don't already know. This will lighten things up and help break the ice.

   As the leader, strive to know everyone's name by the end of every meeting. This will help people feel like they're a part of the group. It will also encourage them to attend future meetings and to volunteer within the organization.

4. **Give people a reason to come to the meeting.** There are so many priorities competing for parents' time. If they think they already know what will be covered during the booster meeting, they may not attend. Here are some pointers to improve the quality of the meeting content:

   - **Create an agenda in advance and stick to it.** Throughout the course of the meeting, allow people to contribute, but diplomatically keep the discussion on topic if you see it starting to stray.
   - **Don't just read information that parents can gather from a website or email.** When sharing items on the calendar of events, provide background details about each activity and tell

them how they can help. Make parents feel like they are getting inside information by attending booster meetings.

- **Update performance to financial goals.** Share the current progress toward the budget and solicit feedback if you are trending away from meeting your goal. People are most engaged when they feel as if they are part of the solution.

- **Ask a student to perform or speak.** If your organization supports the performing arts, give a student or group the opportunity to perform for the parents. They will love to hear from the students, and this will provide a "dress rehearsal" opportunity for students preparing to compete in a contest or festival.

    If your organization supports an athletic team, ask a student to say a few words about a lesson he or she has learned on or off the field. Parents love to hear inspiring stories from the students, and this will reinforce the need for parent involvement and support.

5. **Encourage interaction.** Create an informal setting so that parents feel free to join in the dialogue. Ask the committee chairs to give updates of their activities, but let them know in advance if they need to prepare special information.

6. **Recognize the contributions of others.** Show volunteers your appreciation for their service, but be careful not to leave anyone out. Remember the

basics we learned in chapter seven for motivating others by showing recognition and gratitude.

7. **Respect the time.** Start the meeting on time and try to cover all agenda items within forty-five minutes. After the business meeting, allow time for parents to mingle. When the parents develop personal friendships with one another, they have additional reasons to participate, and their commitment to the organization increases. I have heard many stories of longstanding friendships that were established while serving in booster organizations.

Prioritize and protect the time for parents to mingle after meetings. I once heard of a young instructor who would turn out half the lights in the room, insinuating that it was time to leave. This may be effective with students, but it is just plain rude to the parents who provide the program's support and resources.

8. **Summarize the decisions.** Make sure that everyone understands the decisions that have been made during the meeting and that the secretary has recorded them accurately. Also, repeat any important calls to action so parents will keep them top of mind as they adjourn.

9. **Solicit feedback.** Continuously improve your meeting leadership skills throughout the course of the year. Find a trusted friend who will give you honest and constructive feedback and then hone your style for greater impact during future meetings.

Executive leaders, booster meetings are your time to interact with your core group of volunteers. Put forth the effort to make each meeting a meaningful experience for all who participate. You will know that you have hit the mark when parents apologize to you for missing your meeting!

Leadership Essential #13: Booster meetings are the executive leader's opportunity to energize the core group of volunteers.

FOURTEEN

Sustain the Momentum

Leaders don't create followers, they create more leaders.

– Tom Peters

Now that you have gotten the year off to a great start, it's time to focus on succession planning. Succession planning will help sustain the momentum that you have achieved once your leadership term is complete. This is an area where many booster organizations struggle, and it's likely to keep instructors up at night. The most important part of succession planning is to do it. When you do, you will pave the way for a seamless transition of leadership at the end of the year.

It is important to remember that future booster leaders will bear the responsibility for the success of their organization. Notice that I said "their organization." As a general rule, parents should rotate out of leadership roles when their children graduate. Some organizations have even written this into their bylaws. Since current parents have the most vested interest in the program, you do not want to deny them the opportunity to serve.

So what can you do to facilitate a seamless transition of leadership? Here are six suggestions:

1. **Identify future leaders early.** During one of the year's first executive team meetings, take a look at your roster of officers and committee chairs. Identify those who you know will rotate out at the end of the year – parents of seniors and others who do not plan to return to their current roles. For each of the roles that you have identified, appoint an apprentice to work alongside the current leader. Remember to "recruit in the zone" where a person's passion and strengths intersect. For a refresher on recruiting, refer back to chapter six.

Committee Chair Planning			
Committee	Current Chair	Prospect	Confirmed?
Band Camp Care	Janet Walker	Incumbent	
Band Office Assistant	Jodi Taggert	Incumbent	Yes
Banquet	Melanie Carr		
Bus Chaperones	Karen Wright	Janie Kerr	Yes
Concert	Richard Anders		
Finance	Mary Pratt	Catherine Pineiro	
Forms	Laverne Rice	Heather Brink	Yes
Fundraising - Coupon Book Sale	Kathryn Jones	June Fitzpatrick	
Fundraising - Fruit Sale	Kimberly Britt	Incumbent	Yes
Fundraising - Grocery Gift Card Program	Steven Zuber	Mark White	Yes
Fundraising - NFL Merchandise Sales	James Webb		
Fundraising - University Concessions	Dale Stewart		
Hospitality	Joan Rudolph	Incumbent	Yes
Merchandising	Carol Dean	Incumbent	Yes
Trip	Stephanie Watson		
Truck & Equipment	Steve Carr	Greg Sampson	
Outside Hospitality	Clifford Jackson	Incumbent	
Uniforms	Carrie Novick	Sarah Teel	Yes
Video/Photo	Michelle Holland	Terry Barnes	Yes
Note: Shading indicates current chair will not return.			

Appoint apprentices in time for them to experience the major activities in the roles they will assume. For example, if your organization serves a marching band, appoint an apprentice to work with the Uniforms Committee chair during the football season.

2. **Create ad hoc positions for detail-intensive roles.** In chapter eleven, I shared with you that the Blaze Band Boosters created an ad hoc Finance Committee of one to eventually replace the outgoing treasurer. We recruited a parent with experience in accounting and finance to spend the year working with the current treasurer. At the end of the year, the Finance Committee chair was elected treasurer and seamlessly transitioned into the role.

3. **Schedule hand-off meetings.** When it is time to transition, schedule meetings for outgoing leaders to "hand off" their roles to the incoming replacements. Here the new leaders will receive important documentation and learn the fundamental processes of their new roles. Be intentional in scheduling these meetings, and don't assume that they will happen on their own.

4. **Document procedures.** Succession planning in a booster organization extends beyond the replacement and transition of volunteer labor. Whenever possible, create detailed, written procedures for all leadership roles. I realize that this is labor intensive, and roles are subject to change through the years. However, well-documented procedures will pay huge dividends and ensure continuity throughout the transition of leadership.

5. **Save communications and records.** If you cannot document a procedure for every leadership role, be sure you save copies of communications and records. Typical communications are those sent to all families with program registration information,

student fee requirements, fundraising information, and announcements of booster meetings. Typical records include any reports that you provide to the school board, contracts with fundraising partners, and insurance policies.

6. **Save files to a central location.** To easily access your procedures, communications, and records, consider using a cloud-based storage service like Dropbox. This free service allows authorized users to store and share files in real time. Within the application, set up a logical set of folders categorized by officer's role, committee chair, etc. While you are at it, establish archive folders for prior years' information that can be accessed for file and reference.

To recap, succession planning helps the organization ensure a seamless transition of leadership between school years. Although commonly overlooked by many booster organizations, succession planning can be achieved by recruiting apprentices for future leadership roles and by documenting procedures, communications, and records.

Leadership Essential #14: Succession planning enables the organization to sustain the momentum through the transition of leadership.

PART THREE

THE FINANCE LEADER

FIFTEEN

Comply with the IRS

In the late 1990's a new funding model for booster organizations swept the nation in popularity – individual student accounts. Scout troops, independent athletic teams, and other student support organizations quickly jumped on the bandwagon and implemented student accounts. Based on the premise of individual accountability, student accounts offered several benefits to booster leaders and proactive families alike.

Here's how it worked. The booster organization divided its annual budgeted income by the number of students in the program. This represented the "fair share" each student was expected to contribute. Students worked fundraising events, sold products, and paid out-of-pocket to reach their fair share. Fundraising proceeds were dispersed into student accounts based on participation. The more that students worked or sold, the more proceeds went into their accounts. Families could also bypass fundraisers altogether and pay the full fair share out-of-pocket.

Booster leaders and instructors benefitted from student accounts. Annual budgets were easier to achieve, as students were held accountable for their fair shares. Students who were not current with their accounts were often denied participation in the program. At the end of the school year, it was common to withhold students' grades if they had outstanding debts.

Student accounts provided an incentive for proactive families as funds above and beyond the current year's fair share rolled over to the following year. Funds could also be applied toward the program's annual trip or other event.

Sounds like a great model, right? Well, don't jump too soon. Here's why...

Enter the Internal Revenue Service

The IRS allows booster organizations and other nonprofits to operate tax-exempt under section 501(c)(3). This section establishes stringent guidelines for nonprofits, including, "none of its earnings may inure to any private shareholder or individual."[23] Inure means "to become beneficial or advantageous."[24] Therefore, a booster organization may not allocate funding in a manner that would benefit any individual student over the other students in the program. Funding must be distributed equally to all students, regardless of their individual level of participation in fundraising activities. Furthermore, no student may be denied the opportunity to participate in an extracurricular program based on his or her ability to participate in fundraising.

In 2008, three booster organizations near Lexington, Kentucky learned a difficult lesson about student accounts. After a series of tax audits, the IRS fined the Bryan Station Baseball Boosters $61,000. To put this into perspective, their annual budget was $44,000. The Henry Clay Band Boosters were fined $30,000, and the Lafayette High School Band Boosters $9,000. The infraction? These booster organizations dispersed funds into student accounts according to student participation in fundraisers. Therefore, some students received greater benefit than others in the program. Additionally, these fundraising disbursements reduced the annual fees (fair share) required of each student, which could have exposed families to IRS fines because fundraising credits can be considered as income.[25]

Why is This Important to the IRS?

The IRS's primary function is to generate revenue for the federal government. Since section 501(c)(3) exempts booster organizations from paying taxes, the IRS leaves a considerable amount of revenue "on the table." Without the exemption, you could owe 15 ~ 25% of your organization's income in taxes. When you think in these terms, the IRS's stringent guidelines begin to seem more reasonable.

But it doesn't stop there. Let's illustrate additional tax implications associated with student accounts. Consider that a booster organization sets a fair share of $300 per student. Tyler's family writes a $300 check to satisfy his fair share at the beginning of the year. Megan, on the other hand, works fundraising events through a partnership with the local university. Throughout the course of the year, Megan earns enough through fundraising to satisfy her fair share.

Tyler's family paid out-of-pocket with funds that had already been taxed. Assuming a tax rate of 20%, Tyler's family had already paid $60 in federal income tax on the funds used to satisfy his fair share. Since Megan's fair share was earned through fundraising, the university had most likely made a donation to the booster organization and claimed it as a tax deduction. Therefore, taxes were never collected on the funds used to satisfy Megan's fair share, which we have estimated to be $60.

What Should Booster Organizations Do?

Booster organizations should take advantage of the tax-exemption offered by the IRS under section 501(c)(3). The booster leader's top financial priority is to operate in full compliance with the guidelines provided by the IRS. I am neither an attorney nor an accountant. However, I have learned these five essentials while leading a booster organization:

1. **Operate with one general fund.** This is an absolute requirement. All income shall be deposited into this fund, and all expenses shall be paid from it.

2. **Do not keep records on the side.** Beware of keeping records that could give the appearance that special benefit is given to any student. These records could include hours students worked in fundraisers, points awarded to students for participation in fundraisers, or credit for dollars that students brought into the organization.

3. **Keep records according to sound accounting practices.** Under many funding models, families will make student payments to the organization. You must keep accurate records of all incoming and outgoing funds – that's just good business sense. Occasionally, a parent will want to confirm that a check has been received by the organization.

However, do not use these records to give preferential treatment to any student.

4. **Hire a Certified Public Accountant.** I recommend that all booster organizations keep an accountant on retainer. An accountant will bring expertise to the table and will be able to steer the organization in the right direction. As booster leaders rotate into and out of the organization, the accountant will provide continuity in financial leadership. Have your accountant review the organization's books quarterly or semi-annually, and ask her to help you file financial documents required by the IRS, the state government, and the school board.

5. **When in doubt, seek legal counsel.** At times you will need a legal opinion to help determine an appropriate course of action. As a leader, your peace of mind will far outweigh the cost of an attorney's services. Be sure to select an attorney who specializes in nonprofit operations.

Where Should an Organization Start?

The IRS offers a number of online resources to help an organization achieve and maintain nonprofit status. The Life Cycle of a Public Charity[26] is one of the most beneficial. Here is my assessment of the process steps and their impact to a booster organization.

Starting Out

- **Organizing Documents.** In order to become a 501(c)(3) nonprofit, a booster organization must first incorporate as a legal entity through its state government. Additionally, the organization must have a charter that clearly states its purpose and powers, and a plan to distribute the organization's assets should it dissolve.
- **Bylaws.** The organization's bylaws should define its fiscal, or tax, year.
- **Employer Identification Number (EIN).** This is a unique number used by the IRS to identify the organization. The organization must have an EIN even if it will not hire employees.
- **Charitable Solicitation.** Organizations that intend to solicit funds must first register with their state governments. This registration is important to differentiate you from fundraising scams (for example, those offering relief after natural disasters and other tragic events). You must also register with your state government if you intend to sponsor a raffle or other gaming event.

Applying to the IRS

- **Requirements for Exemption.** According to the IRS, "to be tax-exempt under section 501(c)(3) of the Internal Revenue Code, an organization must be organized and operated exclusively for exempt purposes set forth in section 501(c)(3), and none of its earnings may inure to any private shareholder or individual."[27]

Required Filings

- **Annual Exempt Organization Return.** Once an organization achieves nonprofit status, it must show every year that it continues to operate as a nonprofit. This is typically reported using the 990 family of tax return forms. It is important to note that if an organization fails to file a tax return for three consecutive years, it will automatically lose its tax-exempt status. As officers rotate into and out of roles, it is critical to maintain continuity in tax reporting.

Ongoing Compliance

- **Jeopardizing Exemption.** There are several risks that may jeopardize an organization's tax-exempt status. The most relevant risk to a booster organization is the unequal distribution of funds that would provide benefit to an individual student over other students in the organization. The IRS dedicates a web page to risks that jeopardize exemption.[28]
- **Employment Taxes.** While most booster organizations do not hire employees, many bring in short-term contract labor. Examples include camp instructors and bus drivers. As a hiring entity, the booster organization must provide contract

employees 1099 statements to report the income they earned.

- **Substantiation and Disclosure.** In order for a donor to deduct a charitable contribution of $250 or more, the organization must provide a written acknowledgement of the gift. The IRS offers instructions and resources to help you meet these requirements.
- **Public Disclosure Requirements.** Documentation and annual returns that a nonprofit files with the IRS must be made available to the public upon request.

Significant Events

- **Audits of Exempt Organizations.** The IRS reserves the right to examine a nonprofit organization's returns and analyze its operational and financial activities.

The opportunity for a booster organization to operate without paying taxes is a tremendous financial benefit to the organization. Along with this benefit comes the responsibility to operate within the guidelines set forth by the IRS. We have seen the consequences suffered by the organizations in Lexington, Kentucky, and we have learned how to keep from making those mistakes in the future. Although the general fund financial model does not offer the same accountability as student accounts, it is the required model. Prudent booster leaders will lead their organizations with integrity, playing by the rules in good faith.

Disclaimer: The information provided above is based upon my own practical experience leading a booster organization. I am neither an attorney nor an accountant. If your organization needs financial advice or other expert assistance, seek the services of a competent professional.

Leadership Essential #15: A booster organization must distribute funds equally to all students, regardless of their individual participation in fundraising activities.

Leadership Essential #16: No student may be denied the opportunity to participate in an extracurricular program based on his or her ability to participate in fundraising.

SIXTEEN

Segregate Financial Duties

Search the web for "school booster embezzlement" and you will find more than 100,000 heartbreaking stories of booster volunteers who betrayed their organizations' trust and misappropriated funds for their own personal use. Their devastating acts left their successors to not only replace the financial coffers, but to also rebuild financial integrity and trust of students, parents, school administrators, and the community. Here are a just few examples where these criminals helped themselves to staggering sums of cash:

- In Michigan, a former athletic booster treasurer confessed to embezzling $98,588 from the organization.[29]
- In California, a former band booster president pleaded guilty to embezzling more than $50,000 of the organization's funds.[30]
- In New York, a former booster club treasurer admitted to stealing in excess of $20,000 from the club's accounts.[31]

Booster embezzlement is a crime that is widespread among organizations from coast to coast. Behind each incident you will find several common factors. Here are four:

1. **The perpetrator was in a position of trust.** Let's face it; volunteers are hard to come by. All too often, the majority of a booster organization's tasks

fall upon the shoulders of a core group of volunteers. It is no wonder that organizations are quick to accept volunteers who raise their hands for leadership roles. However, a prudent organization will get to know its volunteers before electing them to office.

Before you put new volunteers in positions of trust, ask yourself, what skills does the volunteer bring to the role? Does the volunteer work in the field of finance? Is the volunteer a manager within his or her company? Has anyone worked alongside this volunteer in prior extracurricular organizations?

It is important to be proactive in recruiting. Never enter into nominations or an election without first reaching out to potential volunteers. This will allow them time to fully consider the commitment they are being asked to make. It will also help to minimize the risk to the organization of accepting someone who may not be well suited for the role.

2. **The perpetrator did not have a criminal past.** Embezzlement is a crime that entices its culprit as opportunities arise. Although you have taken steps to screen volunteer leaders, some may fall to temptation if the conditions are right. Fraud prevention experts commonly refer to the "10-10-80 rule" in categorizing potential thieves. Supposedly, "10 percent of people will never steal, no matter what, 10 percent of people will steal at any opportunity, and the other 80 percent... will go either way depending on how they rationalize a particular opportunity."[32]

Pastor and author Bill Hybels defines character as, "who you are when no one's looking."[33] Access to funds with few restrictions often exposes one's true character, and may result in financial loss to the organization.

3. **Embezzlement happens over time, not in one incident.** Embezzlement is a crime of "erosion" rather than one of "explosion." The erosion often begins with a small, isolated theft. Over time, theft becomes more frequent and for larger amounts. Some perpetrators may justify their actions by thinking they are "borrowing" funds to make it through hard times, or to offset the hours they put in as volunteers.

4. **The perpetrator was operating independently.** A lack of internal controls often gives one individual financial authority over the organization's funds. This autonomy may lead to temptation that is too great to resist. Assuming that no one will find out, many perpetrators build the courage to take that first dollar, then another, and another. It is critically important to ensure that no individual has unsupervised access to the organization's funds.

How Can a Booster Organization Insulate Itself from Embezzlement?

The best way to prevent theft and fraud is to make it difficult to commit theft and fraud. Sounds simple, doesn't it? Well, as simple as it sounds, this is where many booster organizations fail. They do not build proper checks and balances into their operating procedures.

Transparency is the foundation of a booster organization's financial integrity. Therefore, separate financial roles and reporting among two or more people. Auditors refer to this as segregation, or separation, of duties. This is such an important concept that I'm including the full BusinessDictionary.com[34] definition.

Separation of Duties

1. *Control policy according to which no person should be given responsibility for more than one related function. For example, the person responsible for purchasing should not also be responsible for its payment. Also called segregation of duties.*

2. *Methods and procedures established as an internal check on activities through separation of (1) custody of assets from accounting personnel, (2) authorization of transactions from custody of associated assets, and (3) operational responsibilities from record-keeping responsibilities.*

Here are five best practices to help booster organizations segregate financial duties:

1. **Split financial duties between two officers, a treasurer and a bookkeeper.** The Blaze Band Boosters established these two financial roles several years ago. It was a wise move that instilled

financial integrity into the organization. Here's how the duties are divided:

- **Income.** The treasurer receives all incoming checks, maintains a register showing their receipt, and deposits them into the booster's bank account. The treasurer then gives bank deposit records to the bookkeeper to enter into the organization's accounting software program (Intuit QuickBooks[35]).

- **Expenses.** The treasurer receives invoices and check requests, and writes checks from the booster's account to pay them. The treasurer shares the check register with the bookkeeper who assigns expenses to appropriate ledger accounts within QuickBooks.

- **Reporting.** Each month, the treasurer receives the hard copy bank statement and reconciles the check register. The bookkeeper receives the monthly on-line statement, and reconciles QuickBooks records. The bookkeeper also provides a monthly report to the booster executive team, parents, and school administrators, as indicated in item five, below.

2. **Elect financial officers from a pool of volunteers with accounting, finance, or bookkeeping experience.** Many parents have financial training or experience in their background. Understanding the "language" of finance is a critical pre-requisite for the financial officer. From this basic understanding, the volunteer will quickly learn your organization's specific financial operations,

and may also recommend opportunities to continuously improve those operations.

3. **Hire a Certified Public Accountant to review the organization's financial records.** In chapter fifteen, we learned that an accountant will provide sound financial advice, help provide continuity of financial leadership, review the organization's books, and assist in filing documents with the IRS, state government, and the school board. The bookkeeper is typically the primary interface between the organization and the accountant.

4. **Require two signatures on each check written from the booster account.** Authorize two to four officers to sign booster checks, and require two of them to sign each check. Have the officers sign the checks together. While it may seem convenient for an officer to sign several blank checks in advance (for the treasurer to write at a future date), doing so overrides this "check and balance." People of integrity will understand the reason for two signatures, and will want to sign checks together to protect themselves from any suspicion of wrongdoing. For even greater control, only authorize one financial officer – either the treasurer or the bookkeeper – to sign booster checks. This will prevent the opportunity for them to cooperate in fraudulent acts.

5. **Provide monthly financial reports to the executive team, parents, and school administrators.** The monthly financial report

simply shows the beginning booster account balance, income received, expenses paid, and the month-end account balance. Parents deserve transparency to the organization's financial status. Some school boards require booster organizations to submit monthly financial reports. If yours does not, go ahead and provide them this information. It will help build "brand equity" for your organization. Here's an example monthly financial report.

Humes High School Band Boosters - Monthly Financial Report

School Year: 2012~2013	President:	Dan Caldwell
Month of: November, 2012	Treasurer:	Melanie Carr

1. Beginning account balance, as of: 11/1/12	$	36,778.45

2. Income:

a. Fundraiser: University concessions	$	1,042.42
b. Fundraiser: Fruit sales	$	3,414.00
c. Fundraiser: Grocery gift card program	$	547.37
d. Fundraiser: Business sponsorship program	$	700.00
e. Donation	$	100.00
Total revenue for the month:	$	5,803.79

3. Expenses:

a. Football band expenses (see itemized list)	$	1796.03
b. Sheet music	$	2016.11
c. Booster operating expenses (copier & postage)	$	141.80
d. Fundraiser expenses (PayPal)	$	319.08
e. Refunds for student payments (withdrawn)	$	300.00
Total expenditures for the month:	$	4,573.02

4. Ending account balance, as of: 11/30/12	$	38,009.22

Dan Caldwell	12/1/12
President's Signature	Date
Melanie Carr	12/1/12
Treasurer's Signature	Date

What Else Can a Booster Organization Do to Ensure Financial Integrity?

In addition to segregating financial duties, here are seven additional opportunities to ensure financial integrity:

1. **Partner with your bank to prevent theft and fraud.** Many booster organizations' budgets are comparable to those of small businesses. Therefore, banks often competitively pursue booster organizations' business. Carefully select a bank that understands the needs of a nonprofit – preferably booster – organization and is willing to stand beside you as a partner. Select a bank with a branch manager who is willing to be your central point of contact. In the spirit of transparency, each authorized officer should establish a professional relationship with the bank's branch manager. Here are a few tips to maximize your partnership with your bank:

   • **Promptly transfer authority to newly elected officers.** A booster officer's greatest authority is to control financial activities. Therefore, the first task for newly elected officers is to promptly transition authority with the bank. This protects both the outgoing officers and the incoming officers.

   • **Always pay with a booster check and avoid reimbursements.** Prior to making a purchase, have the buyer request a booster check from the treasurer made out to the appropriate vendor for the purchase amount. Do not allow people to make out-of-pocket purchases and request a reimbursement later. Booster expenditures should be budgeted and planned. Allowing out-of-pocket purchases contributes to impulse buying and increases the potential for purchases with lost receipts.

- **Always issue checks in sequence.** This is a best practice that will help prevent the misappropriation of a check for an individual's benefit. When checks are haphazardly issued, it becomes difficult to keep track of them all. Likewise, when checks are issued in sequence, they should clear the bank in the same relative sequence. This discipline allows for prompt investigation if an abnormality is discovered.

- **Do not authorize instructors to sign booster checks.** Elected booster officers are responsible to oversee the organization's funds. Instructors should not handle any funds, period. There are at least three benefits to this policy. First, it eliminates the opportunity for an instructor to give in to temptation and misappropriate funds for personal gain. Second, the executive team will have greater visibility to the program's expenditures. Third, the instructor will be protected from suspicion of wrongdoing by this "arm's length" relationship.

- **Select a bank that will enforce two signatures to authorize a check.** As we've discussed, two booster officers are required to authorize every check. It is important that your bank stand beside you on this requirement. When the Blaze Band Boosters first implemented the two-signature rule, there were a couple of checks that inadvertently went out with only one signature. Our bank upheld the two-signature rule and did not clear the checks against the account. This accidental oversight actually demonstrated the strength of our partnership with the bank.

- **Select a bank that will protect you from external theft.** Thus far, we have addressed the issue of theft and fraud from within. Your bank can also help to protect you against theft from outside the organization. Here's a real life example. In the midst of a hectic day, our treasurer mailed the payment for a booster invoice from her home mailbox. She placed the letter in the box, raised the flag, and left home to run an errand. Rather than signaling the mailman to pick up the letter, the mailbox flag signaled a thief to steal the letter before the mailman arrived. The thief "washed" our check to remove the ink, then went for a $2500 shopping spree at Walmart. In the checkout lane, the cashier printed the check for the purchase amount, and then returned the voided check to the thief. This electronic transfer kept the actual check from returning to the bank. Later, the thief returned the merchandise for a cash refund at customer service.

Our bank stood by us in this predicament, and took charge of the investigation. Most important for us, they did not withdraw $2500 from our account. They coordinated with Walmart and local authorities to identify and prosecute the thief.

Our bank's customer service through this incident reinforced their commitment to our partnership. We developed a much deeper appreciation for their role as our financial ally. And, we all learned to never mail a check from our home mailbox!

2. **Institute a "no cash" policy.** If your school system does not already prohibit you from accepting cash, institute this policy on your own. Cash is the least secure method for a booster organization to conduct its financial transactions. Here are a few risks that cash presents to an organization:

- **Cash is "liquid."** Cash is accepted everywhere. Because it is not traceable, stolen cash may be spent without question.
- **Cash increases the potential for theft.** Even with the best safeguards in place, vulnerable volunteers, both adults and students, may be tempted to steal.
- **Cash transactions may be inaccurately documented, or not documented at all.** Receipts must accompany all cash transactions. If a mistake is made, it is very difficult to identify the inaccurate receipt. Additionally, a dishonest

volunteer may intentionally neglect to give a receipt and keep the incoming cash.

- **Invoices may be falsified in order to cover up a fraudulent payment of cash.** Outgoing cash may be easily diverted to a dishonest volunteer by creating a false invoice to account for the transaction.

The advantages of a "no cash" policy extend beyond the risk of theft. The Blaze Band Booster funding model requests a student payment prior to band camp each year. A parent new to the organization once claimed to have sent $75 in cash with her daughter on the opening morning of band camp. The parent claimed to have run out of checks, so she sent cash instead. This turned out to be a calculated move on her part, as she realized how hectic the first day of band camp would be for the band directors and volunteers. Because cash cannot be traced, and she claimed to have sent it on one of the busiest days of the year, she wagered that the booster executive team would assume the error was on our side. However, we stood behind our clearly stated "no cash" policy. She later sent a check for the outstanding amount.

3. **If cash is inherent to a fundraiser, handle it securely and promptly.** Many booster organizations work concession stands and other events where cash is received from customers. In this case, be prudent with the handling and security of the cash. Designate two people to count the cash and prepare the bank deposit. Have them both sign

off on the bank deposit slip. Deposit the cash into the bank as soon as possible – no later than 24 hours after the event. Here's a best practice – if you work concessions for a game with police security, ask an officer to accompany you to the bank to make the deposit. This will help ensure your personal safety, and it will enhance transparency and speed in the cash handling process.

4. **Provide a secure deposit box in the classroom or locker room.** Throughout the school year, students will turn in proceeds from fundraisers, student payments, and other documentation to the boosters. You can eliminate the administrative burden on your instructor by constructing or purchasing a locked deposit box and centrally locating it in the classroom or locker room. Students deposit their correspondence into the box during the school day. The treasurer collects correspondence from the box, which allows the instructor to maintain an "arm's length" relationship to the booster organization's financial affairs.

5. **Purchase fidelity bond insurance.** Booster organizations may purchase a fidelity bond, which is an insurance product that protects the organization from fraudulent and dishonest acts of its volunteers.[36]

6. **Save or back up financial records to "the cloud."** To increase transparency, copy the organization's financial records to a cloud-based storage service, such as Dropbox.[37] This will provide the executive team visibility to check registers,

electronic bank statements, monthly financial reports, QuickBooks backups, and other financial files. It will also provide a backup in the event that the original files become electronically corrupt.

7. **Retain records in accordance with IRS requirements and standard accounting practices.** An organization's records tell its financial story over a defined period of time. If your booster organization becomes subject to a school board, IRS, or other regulatory agency's audit, you will be required to present detailed financial records. Your accountant will advise you which records to retain as well as the appropriate retention period for those records. At the end of the retention period, destroy the records. Although conventional wisdom may be to hold records beyond their retention period, it may not be advantageous to do so. Again, your accountant will advise you on accepted records destruction practices.

In this chapter, we have seen the unfortunate reality that embezzlement is a crime that is widespread among booster organizations across the country. These criminals typically operate independently over an extended period of time. The best defense for an organization is to establish a transparent system of internal controls. Divide financial roles and responsibilities among volunteers to segregate the duties. Consider your bank a partner to help you prevent both internal and external theft. Also, institute a "no cash" policy, provide a secure deposit box in the classroom or locker room, purchase fidelity bond insurance, and maintain records in accordance with specified retention schedules.

Leadership Essential #17: Transparent operating procedures are the foundation of a booster organization's financial integrity.

Leadership Essential #18: Separate financial roles and reporting between two or more people.

Leadership Essential #19: Partner with your bank to prevent internal and external theft and fraud.

SEVENTEEN

Develop a Comprehensive Budget

A budget is the financial roadmap for a booster organization, and the executive team develops it. Your budget should be zero-based, meaning that income minus expenses equals zero. The budget is your tool to show parents and school administrators how much income it will take to operate the program and where the income will be spent.

When developing a budget, the executive team forecasts expenses and income for the upcoming year. The goal in budgeting is to accurately predict expenses and income. Under ideal conditions, actual expenses and income will equal what you have budgeted. If you encounter unbudgeted expenses throughout the year, you may have to increase your income to make ends meet. This will be unpopular among your parents, as they may have to fundraise or contribute additional funds.

While it may seem beneficial to end the year with a surplus (to have not spent all of your income), this creates its own issues. First, parents may begin to question why they were asked to contribute and fundraise as much as they did. Second, a nonprofit organization is exactly that – not for profit. If you end with a surplus two or three years in a row, you're likely to raise the curiosity of regulating authorities. If you see in the fourth quarter you're on track to end with a surplus, don't stockpile cash. Roll the surplus back into the program to benefit the students. The surplus could be used to reduce the following year's student payments or to purchase equipment and supplies that did not get approved for the current year's budget.

As an executive team, be intentional when budgeting and strive for accuracy.

Start Here

It is best to begin the budgeting process late in the third quarter of the fiscal year. This will give you time to review, revise, and approve your budget before the new year begins. The first step is to reflect on your performance to the current year's budget. Here are a couple of questions to consider in your reflection activity:

- **Are you achieving your budget by your actions, or are other factors contributing to your favorability?** If things are running as planned, you should be trending along with your budget. However, you have to look deeper than the bottom line to fully understand what is driving your performance. For example, are your fundraisers generating the income that you forecasted, or did you receive an unexpected gift from a generous donor? Have you spent all that you budgeted, or have you not had to repair or replace equipment as planned? Have variable expenses been low because of a decline in enrollment?

- **Are you doing everything you planned, but not meeting your budget?** If so, you must analyze the cause. Have you conducted your fundraisers, but not realized the proceeds you expected? Have you been able to generate the income you projected from requested student payments? Perhaps you have purchased equipment and supplies as planned, but the price increased since the budget was created.

Create Your Budget

Once you have reflected on your performance to the current budget, you are ready to draft a budget for the upcoming year. It is important to apply the lessons that you have learned to improve the accuracy of your new budget. As you work through the following steps, you may find it helpful to pause and reflect, and take a deeper dive into a particular area.

1. **Identify needs.** Start this process with your instructor's draft. He will have visibility to variables such as forecasted enrollment, changes in school board requirements, and rule modifications within the sport or program area. Additionally, he should have an accurate assessment of the condition of the program's equipment and the need for repair and replacement.

   Next, have the officers contribute their recommendations. Here are a few points of consideration:

   - **Seek the committee chairs' input.** Because the committee chairs are closer to their assigned areas than anyone else in the organization, they will help you identify needs that you may not otherwise see. They will often have ideas for generating additional income as well.

- **Include general and administrative (G&A) expenses.** Examples of G&A expenses are accountant's and attorney's fees, state charter registration fees, insurance premiums, software license renewal fees, and office supplies. If you collect on-line payments through a vendor such as PayPal,[38] be sure to budget for their service charge.

- **Account for pass-through expenses.** Pass-through expenses are expenses encountered by the organization that are offset by their own corresponding income. Examples include cost of goods sold in fundraisers and banquet expenses that will be offset by ticket sales. The income required to operate the Blaze Band Boosters in 2012~2013 was $73,100. However, after adding pass-through expenses, the bottom line grew to $85,200. Be sure to explain this to your parents so that they understand the portion of the income they are being asked to generate ($73,100 in this example).

- **Budget for the instructor's personal development.** Your instructor enriches the students' lives every day. Don't overlook the opportunity to replenish your instructor's creativity and learning. You may cover conference registration fees, purchase books and training materials, or provide trade magazine subscriptions to support your instructor's personal growth. As a note of caution, be sure that you comply with the guidelines of your school board and state and local athletic regulatory agencies. Some of these groups have established rules for instructor development to prevent a program from gaining an unfair competitive advantage.

- **Include the portion of a multi-year initiative.** Does your midterm plan include a capital campaign? If so, reflect the year's portion of the campaign as an expense so that an equivalent, offsetting amount of income will be budgeted as well.

Once you have identified all projected expenses, allocate them to the appropriate months when they will occur. This will serve as a baseline to track your progress each month. Then, tally expenses to determine how much income it will take to fund the year's operations.

2. **Subtract funds budgeted by the school board.** Does your school board fund a portion of your budget? If so, be sure to subtract that from the total income required to fund your program. The difference will be the amount of income the booster organization will have to generate.

3. **Divide by the number of students in the program.** This will give you the cost per student to run the program.

4. **Determine the percentage of income provided by student payments vs. fundraising.** Ideally, all budgeted income would

come from fundraising, with zero out-of-pocket from students and families. However, this is not always feasible. In the budgeting process, determine how many out-of-pocket dollars you will request from each student, and how many dollars fundraising will generate. We'll discuss student payments in chapter eighteen and fundraising in chapter nineteen.

5. **Communicate the budget and funding model to the parents.** This is best done during a booster meeting. Explain the rationale behind the budget and funding model, and encourage discussion. Booster members' feedback may reflect an omission in the budget or identify an error. Have the boosters vote to approve the budget if it is required by your organization's bylaws.

   Additionally, communicate the budget and funding model through other channels, such as newsletters and a link to your website.

6. **Submit the final budget to the school board.** Many school boards require booster organizations to submit their annual budgets. If your school board does not require this, voluntarily submit your budget anyway. This gesture will help you establish a reputation of financial integrity with the school board.

Here's an example budget:

Humes High School Band Boosters - Annual Budget

Treasurer's Signature: _____

Year Beginning: June 2012
Year Ending: May 2013

President's Signature: _____

Income	Jun	Jul	Aug	Sep	Oct	Nov	Dec	Jan	Feb	Mar	Apr	May	TOTAL
Student Payments	$17,000	$17,000											$34,000
Banquet Income											$1,100	$1,100	$2,200
Festivals - Student Payments				$1,700									$1,700
Fundraisers													
Coupon Book			$1,400	$4,500									$5,900
Fruit Sale						$5,200	$4,200						$9,400
University Concessions		$900	$2,200		$1,800		$800	$1,900	$800	$1,400	$1,600		$11,200
NFL Merchandise Booth							$7,200		$2,800				$10,000
Grocery Gift Card Program	$900	$900	$900	$900	$900	$900	$900	$900	$900	$900	$900	$900	$10,800
TOTAL INCOME	$17,900	$18,800	$4,500	$5,400	$4,200	$6,100	$13,100	$2,800	$4,500	$2,300	$3,600	$2,000	$85,200

Expenses	Jun	Jul	Aug	Sep	Oct	Nov	Dec	Jan	Feb	Mar	Apr	May	TOTAL
Functions Expense		$2,030	$600	$200	$1,000	$100	$1,000		$400	$200		$200	$5,700
Operations Expense		$800	$100	$200	$100	$200	$100	$200		$200	$100		$2,300
Banquet Expense												$5,400	$5,400
Concerts				$100				$100			$100		$300
Festivals/Clinics/Honor Bands						$1,000	$1,000	$700	$100		$1,400		$4,200
Football Band		$12,000	$12,000	$7,000	$3,300	$3,000					$100	$4,000	$41,400
Fundraiser Expenses							$3,000	$3,000		$2,000	$400	$500	$8,900
Incidentals				$300									$300
Instructors (non-Football Band)		$1,400								$700		$1,400	$3,500
Instruments/Equipment (non-Football Band)				$200	$200		$400	$200	$300		$600	$7,600	$9,500
Music			$2,100	$200		$400	$700		$300				$3,700
TOTAL EXPENSES	$0	$16,000	$14,800	$8,200	$4,600	$7,700	$6,200	$1,200	$1,100	$3,100	$2,700	$19,600	$85,200

Manage Your Cash Flow

In the world of investments there is a saying, "cash is king." This is true in booster organizations as well. A booster organization must take care of its cash flow. Just because you operate under a zero-based budget doesn't mean that you can end the year with zero cash on hand. For many organizations, the majority of expenses occur at the start of the fiscal year.

As a rule of thumb, an organization should end each year with a balance that will cover half of the following year's expenses. Otherwise, you will not be able to cover start-up expenses at the beginning of the year before fundraising activities begin. Throughout the year, fundraising and student payments will replenish funds that have been spent and will provide for current expenses. Since rules and regulations vary by state and locality, you should seek your accountant's guidance to ensure this is an acceptable practice in your area.

In summary, a budget is the financial roadmap for a booster organization. A comprehensive, accurate budget will serve as a tool to communicate your financial plan to your parents and school administrators, and to measure your financial progress throughout the year. After preparing your budget, maintain your cash flow to cover expenses as they occur throughout the year.

Leadership Essential #20: A comprehensive, accurate budget serves as the financial roadmap for the organization.

EIGHTEEN

Establish Reasonable Student Payments

Now that you have developed your annual budget, let's take a look at generating income to operate the program. But first, remember that the IRS requires funds to be distributed equally among all students, so students bringing zero funds into the organization will receive the same benefit as the top participants. And, you cannot require students to pay fees in order to take part in extracurricular activities.

Many Boards of Education have clearly defined rules for school fees. In the state of Tennessee, "school fees may be requested from but not required of any student, regardless of financial status...[including] fees for activities and supplies required to participate in all courses offered for credit or grade, including interscholastic athletics and marching band if taken for credit..."[39]

Please note that these rules do not prevent an organization from *requesting* fees to operate the program. Because of the sensitivity associated with the word "fees," the Blaze Band Boosters referred to these funds as "student payments."[40] We defined student payments as the portion of the organization's annual budget that you request families to pay out-of-pocket.

Student payments benefit the organization by providing an immediate source of income. At the beginning of the school year, this influx of cash can jump-start the program's operations. It also helps to balance your cash flow, as proceeds earned from fundraising activities typically lag behind the events themselves.

The income contributed by student payments versus that generated by fundraising varies from one organization to another. Factors that influence this proportion include family demographics, student enrollment, volunteer participation, and school board rules and policies. Student payments should be reasonable and fair and established with parents' input.

Remember to factor in uncollected payments when budgeting income to be contributed from student payments. Because you cannot require funds to be paid as a condition of participation, it is unreasonable to assume that you will achieve 100% of your target. In the reflection phase of budgeting, take a look at your current income from student payments to determine what has been uncollected. For example, in 2012~2013 the Blaze Band fell short of its student payment target by 16% due to uncollected payments. Therefore, we increased the 2013~2014 student payment budget to offset this projected shortfall.

Four Best Practices When Collecting Student Payments

Use diplomacy and discretion when collecting your organization's student payments. Here are four best practices:

1. **Do not act as a collection agency.** Remember, you may *request* but not *require* student payments. Let's face it, most families don't budget booster payments along with food, clothing, and shelter.

However, from my experience, a friendly reminder is all it takes to encourage most people to pay. Although email communication is convenient, a personal phone call is much more effective.

I recommend that the executive team develop a standard approach to remind families of payment deadlines. Establish a reminder schedule, and assign each officer families to contact. Create a list of key points so that all families will hear the same message.

When speaking with parents, remind them of the overall income goal for the organization, and share with them the progress to date. For example, "we have achieved 65% of our income goal of $75,000 for the year." Do not quote the percentage of families who have, or have not, met their requested student payment. Remember, you are trying to fulfill one general fund for the organization, and you are encouraging everyone to participate. Do not threaten to deny their child the opportunity to participate in the extracurricular activity. Likewise, do not promise any special benefit for their child if they make their payments. This clearly violates the rules and the essence of a nonprofit organization.

2. **Give the benefit of the doubt.** When you accept a leadership role, you will see who contributes the most and who contributes the least. It is easy to assume that, by default, parents resist participating in their children's activities. While that is true for some parents, it is certainly not true for all. Don't allow yourself to fall into this negative trap. Whether

you realize it or not, it will show in the way you conduct your business.

I learned an important lesson early in my tenure as president. Each year, we sponsored a spring trip that was open to all band students. The trip was fully funded by the participants, outside of the annual budget, and we requested parents to fulfill their student payments before paying trip fees.

Our treasurer sent me a list of the trip participants who had not met the full student payment. I promptly whipped out a series of emails reminding them the importance of meeting the band budget before funding the trip. One of our freshman parents, a single dad, replied that he was not aware of the requested student payment, and it would be difficult to make both the student payment and the trip fee. I simply could not believe that he did not know about the student payment. After all, shouldn't everyone understand how the program is funded and know exactly how to do their part? Well, not in this case.

I learned that he lived out of state, and that his former wife had not shared any details about the booster organization with him. He also wanted to chaperone the trip as a way to spend some time with his son. I was so close to the operation that I failed to look at the organization from the varying perspectives of all parents. I assumed that most parents didn't care about supporting their children's activities, and in this case I was wrong. We did work things out, and we had an enjoyable trip with him and his son. I regret that I took such a strong position before learning the facts, and I changed my approach after that.

3. **Allow alternate payment plans.** Although school fees may not be required for students to participate in the program, I believe that most parents feel an obligation to do their part. Always make provisions for families to arrange alternate payment plans. There is often no visible way to know the financial challenges that some families are facing. Establish alternate payment plans in confidence between one booster officer (typically the treasurer) and the parent. Both parties should agree upon the payment due date. This is good for the parent as it sets a target to work toward.

We recruited one of our best committee chairs through an alternate payment arrangement. When Linda entered the organization, her husband had recently left the family. To make matters worse, the nation was in the middle of an economic crisis that left her without a job. Linda sincerely wanted to do her part, and was an excellent steward of the limited funds coming into her household. She fulfilled her alternate payment commitment right on time. The following year, I asked her to chair one of our fundraisers, and she performed like a champ! I believe that serving as a committee chair boosted her self-esteem and helped her bounce back from the challenges life had put in her way.

4. **Know the facts about tax deductions.** Parents will ask you if they can claim student payments as

tax deductions. Seek the guidance of your attorney before giving advice. Here's the statement that our attorney advised us to include in our documentation:

> We comply with IRS guidelines for nonprofit organizations. Student payments made to the organization are not tax deductible. Any additional contributions to the organization above and beyond these amounts are tax deductible. You should consult with your tax advisor to determine your eligibility to deduct such additional contributions on your federal or state income tax returns.

Student payments provide the opportunity to jump-start a program's operations. Remember to handle student payments sensitively, and never act as a collection agency. Give parents the benefit of the doubt and treat them with respect, as you would want to be treated. Allow alternate payment plans to help those who may be struggling to do their part. And remember, most importantly, you may request but not require student payments.

Leadership Essential #21: Organizations may request but not require student payments.

NINETEEN

Fundraise with Purpose

Wouldn't you love to begin the school year with the assurance of meeting all your fundraising goals? After all, funding is the most tangible sign of support for a program. Let's pull back the curtain and look at the secrets to effective and profitable fundraising.

Fundraising marketers bombard you with promises of extraordinary proceeds that you can generate with minimal effort. Their products, plans, and schemes may seem to yield unbelievable results, but the truth is, if it sounds too good to be true, it is too good to be true.

For the majority of organizations, fundraising is a marathon, not a sprint. The field is crowded with student groups, nonprofits, and other organizations competing for the general public's charitable dollar. So what can you do to achieve your fundraising goals? Tailor your approach. Here are twelve ways to get the highest return from your fundraising efforts:

1. **Limit the number of fundraisers.** This may seem counter intuitive. Conventional wisdom leads you to believe that the more fundraisers you have, the more you will earn. However, it's just the opposite. If you are constantly in fundraising mode, your students and parents will become fatigued and your participation rate will drop. They will not be willing to continually solicit their relatives and neighbors with the "fundraiser of the month." It is

better to conduct a few fundraisers with excellence than many with mediocrity.

2. **Calculate the payout on the front end.** Before committing to a fundraiser, calculate its potential on the "back of the napkin." How will the fundraiser contribute toward your overall fundraising goal? What student participation rate will be considered a success? If the fundraiser involves selling a product, how much will each student need to sell? Is this reasonable?

3. **Carefully select fundraising partners.** New fundraising companies spring up every day so be prudent when selecting a fundraising partner. Ask for references, and actually contact them. Here are a few questions to ask:

- How helpful is the company's customer service?
- Do they ship in a timely manner?
- How is the quality of the product upon delivery, especially if the product is perishable?
- What is their product return policy?

My son's Boy Scout troop once partnered with a fundraising company that promised many incentives and prizes for the boys. The boys sold diligently, each one pushing to the next tier within his reach to earn a better prize. At the end of the sale, the fundraising company did not live up to their promises – they did not fulfill the incentives and prizes the boys earned. Fortunately, they did provide the customers' product, but shipped it to us without any interaction from their sales staff. This experience taught the adult volunteers to carefully select fundraising partners, and it created a teachable moment for the boys about honesty and integrity. And yes, we did pull together some alternate prizes to honor the boys' efforts.

4. **Provide value to your customer.** Ask yourself, is the product or service you are selling something that you would want to buy? Is it reasonably priced? Your customers may not expect the absolute lowest price, but they need to feel like they've received value for their purchase.

   Here's an example of what NOT to do. A recent trend in my town has been for student groups to stand at the entrances to Walmart with buckets asking for donations. DON'T do this! Your customers deserve something in return for their donations, and your students need to learn the value of hard work. When they work to earn the funds that support their program, they'll build pride, ownership, and self-esteem, and they'll learn about free enterprise and capitalism in the process.

5. **Provide excellent customer service.** Excellent customer service makes the difference between a one-time sale and a customer for life. When you are friendly and polite and promptly deliver, you will create repeat business. You'll also build the brand of your booster organization and extracurricular program.

6. **Make it easy for the customer to purchase.** Create order forms that are simple and easy to understand, and make sure that your students have the resources they need to make a sale when a

customer is ready. Sell your product on your website, offering payment through PayPal or another e-commerce service. If you don't have the ability to sell through your website, at least provide sale information, frequently asked questions, and clear instructions for how to buy.

7. **Capitalize on "signature" fundraisers.** A "signature" fundraiser is synonymous with your program, offers proven value to your customers, and generates repeat customers. Here's an example. The Blackman Football Boosters sell a pocket discount card with special offers from local restaurants and businesses. The discounts provide significant value, which generally allow the card to pay for itself within the first month of use. The card is valid for one year, which drives repeat customers. The fundraiser also helps build the brand of the organization, as customers receive value each time they use their Blackman Football Card.

You may also be able to capitalize on a fundraiser that has become popular within your extracurricular activity or sport. For example, high school band programs in the south have sponsored fruit sales for more than thirty years. Customers have become familiar with these sales, and for many it is a tradition to purchase band fruit for the Thanksgiving and Christmas holidays.

8. **Communicate well.** Effective communication is the key to your fundraising success. Send a simple and clear message to your students and parents so they will know what's expected of them. It takes a

while before everyone is "on the same page," so you'll need to repeat the same message several times. Remember from chapter ten, Andy Stanley says that you must repeat your message twenty-one times before people start to hear it.

When communicating with customers, be brief and to the point. Clearly describe the product you are selling and let them know when it will be delivered. Include a clear call to action that will persuade the potential customer to make a purchase.

9. **Frequently report your progress.** When people see progress being made toward a goal, they are more likely to get involved and help achieve the goal. If you do not report your progress, people will lose their motivation to participate and assume that others will meet the goal.

10. **Provide the students an incentive.** It is possible to award your top sellers without violating the essence of the nonprofit. The best way is to award prizes by a drawing. At the start of the fundraiser, establish tiers of participation. As students achieve sales within the tiers, enter their names into the drawing for prizes. This will give students an incentive to sell, but will not award any individual student in proportion to funds earned.

11. **Push the limits with marketing.** Always consider different angles to motivate your students and parents to participate in fundraisers. For example, in a fruit sale, challenge your families to capture the market on fruit, leaving local grocers with fruit spoiling on their shelves. Here's another

example. A local grocery store chain sponsors one of the most profitable fundraisers in our area. Families purchase the store's gift cards and use them to purchase food, pharmacy, and fuel products. When families reload money onto their cards, four percent of the reload amount is paid to the participating nonprofit organization.

Here are some creative ways to market this program to your families:

- Create your own multi-level marketing program by encouraging families to enlist their extended family members and friends.

- Develop a plan to keep seniors engaged in the program beyond graduation.

- Reach out to nonparticipating families through personalized email, highlighting how quickly the benefits add up. Similarly, craft a message for current participants sharing simple strategies to produce greater value for them and to deliver higher proceeds to the organization.

12. **Know your state laws regarding sales tax for products sold.** Although your nonprofit organization is tax-exempt, you may be required to collect and pay state sales tax on the products you sell. Laws vary by state, and some allow a certain number of tax-exempt sales events to be conducted over a defined number of days. Sales tax laws are generally found on your state comptroller's or secretary of state's website. You should seek guidance from your accountant or attorney prior to

the start of any fundraiser to determine your sales tax liability.

These twelve points will help you generate the highest possible proceeds from your fundraisers. When your focus is to provide value and service to your customer, the funds will roll in and before you know it, your goals will be met.

Leadership Essential #22: To meet your fundraising goals, provide value and service to your customer.

TWENTY

Reduce Costs to Boost the Bottom Line

Do what you can, with what you have, where you are.

– Theodore Roosevelt

So far, we have looked at ways to bring income into the organization. Now let's look at the other side of the coin – reducing costs. As leaders, we must be good stewards of the organization's funds and approach our roles with a frugal mindset. But this doesn't mean compromising our standards to save a buck. Our goal is to *effectively* meet every need at the lowest possible cost. For example, you may buy generic bottled water as a frugal alternative to name brand.

Sometimes the lowest cost option simply is not the best option. In the sweltering August heat, both our band and football team take to the practice fields for summer camp. Combined, more than 300 students and volunteers create a demand for ice that well exceeds the school cafeteria's supply. The lowest cost option is to get additional ice from the middle school cafeteria across the street. This literally requires a lot of heavy lifting several times a day. You've also got to assume that the middle school's machines will be able to keep up with the demand. The band booster's executive team considered these risks and the serious health consequences of heat exhaustion, and decided to rent a freezer and have an ice company stock it every day. This was definitely not the cheapest option, but it was the best option for our students and volunteers.

There will be times when you have to make major cuts to control costs. During the economic crisis of 2009, many of our families experienced work slow downs, and some even lost their jobs. To be good stewards of booster funds, we delayed buying replacement instruments and other capital equipment. This helped us through the challenging time, but could only be sustained over the short term. You cannot continually cut costs as a means to achieve your budget. It will only starve the organization, and the program will soon suffer.

Effective cost reduction requires creativity and the commitment to follow through with implementation of your ideas. Here are a few thought starters. Some of them may seem intuitive, and others a bit far fetched. However, they are intended to stretch your imagination and encourage you to explore all opportunities.

1. **Get aggressive with coupons.** Recruit a few savvy shoppers in your organization and put them to work clipping coupons and seeking out sales. Find stores that double the face value of coupons and offer competitive price matching. This is a great way to buy consumable products, such as bottled water, sports drinks, and paper goods.

2. **Take advantage of parents' employee discounts.** Do some of your parents work in industries that supply goods you need to run your program? If so, explore the opportunity to buy those

goods with their employee discounts. One of our parents worked for a local bottling company. He volunteered to purchase bottled water and sports drinks at his discounted rate, up to the full quantity he was allowed each month. Over a period of four months, he could accumulate enough drinks to meet the program's needs for the entire football season.

3. **Publish electronic newsletters.** Many organizations mail paper newsletters and other communications to their families. You can email your newsletter to reduce administrative and postage expenses. You'll also reduce the need for volunteer labor to print and prepare newsletters for mailing. If you are concerned that not everyone will receive your communications, you can always offer to mail paper newsletters to families who prefer home delivery.

4. **Rent equipment instead of buying it.** If you need a trailer or ATV for a limited time during the year, consider renting instead of buying. When deciding whether to rent or buy, be sure to include maintenance in the cost of ownership, as well as deterioration of tires and other consumable parts. If you are unsure if a piece of equipment will meet your needs, rent for a while as a trial. Then you'll know what will best fit your needs.

5. **Sponsor Boy Scout Eagle service projects.** If you have Boy Scouts in your program or school, consider sponsoring an Eagle Scout service project. The scout will manage all aspects of the project, including design, funding, and leadership of

volunteer labor. An Eagle Scout in the Blaze Band led the construction of a 30-foot tall wooden tower at the band's practice field. From the tower, band directors have visibility over the entire field, which helps them guide students through the halftime show formations during practice.

6. **Evaluate your insurance policy coverage.** Do you have a parent who works in the insurance industry? If so, ask her to evaluate your insurance policies. We were able to save a small amount from our annual premium by canceling terrorism coverage. The coverage applied only to events of $5 million or more, and paid benefits after the Federal Government covered the first 85% of the cost. We were confident that we had been over insured.

7. **Trade equipment with other school groups.** When you need equipment, reach out to other school groups and ask if they have anything to trade. Do not wait to see what shows up on the countywide equipment disposal list – make a specific request to a targeted group. For example, if a band's preliminary enrollment calls for an additional tuba, ask the band director to contact her peers at other schools and negotiate a trade. She may be even more strategic by targeting a program with a projected decrease in enrollment.

8. **Pursue quantity discounts when purchasing uniforms.** There is power in numbers, and vendors often offer volume discounts for the additional business. If you are in the market for uniforms, find out if any other schools' teams are also replacing

theirs. You may be able to place the two orders with the same vendor for a volume discount. This is one time when you and your competitor can win together.

You may explore another opportunity with vendors that sell uniforms for many sports. If you combine orders with a team of another sport, you may be able to negotiate a volume discount. This may be especially helpful for teams within your school. Assuming both programs launched when the school first opened, you have a good chance of being on the same uniform replacement cycle.

9. **Be creative.** Think beyond conventional boundaries when seeking ways to reduce costs. Here's an idea to push the boundaries. I know and understand that coaches are as protective of their sports fields as momma bears are of their cubs. However, all schools in your area have to maintain their fields. Is it really necessary for every school to have its own mowing and field maintenance equipment? Could schools share equipment? Could field maintenance be planned around schools' home and away schedules? While this may not be a popular suggestion, it is intended to make you think of the possibilities when you look beyond conventional boundaries.

In summary, these are just a few ideas to help you brainstorm effective ways to reduce your costs. Ask your parents for their cost savings ideas. I'll bet you'll find many of them have great ideas and are willing to help out with implementation.

Leadership Essential #23: The frugal leader effectively meets every need at the lowest possible cost.

TWENTY-ONE

Minimize Your Risk

We've just taken an in-depth look at the effort it takes to generate income for your organization. Through the years, those hard-earned dollars have brought equipment into your program, and you work very hard to keep it properly maintained. You would never take an unreasonable risk that could leave you with a costly repair bill. However, you may be unaware of one of your greatest, hidden risks – operating without insurance.

Insurance is one of those expenses that is easy for a volunteer staff to overlook when budgeting. Since you support a school program, you may assume that your activities are covered by the school's insurance policy. However, regulations vary from state to state. Chances are you'll need your own insurance.

To begin, meet with an insurance agent you trust and describe all of your organization's activities. Assess the risk of each activity and determine if you need insurance. Then, estimate the level of coverage that will reduce each risk.

Here are a few common activities that you should insure to protect your organization from loss:

1. **Transporting equipment and uniforms.** When you travel to other schools for games and special events, you should insure both the act of transportation and the property that you take with you.

First, let's consider transportation. Many booster organizations own trailers, and volunteers pull them behind their personal vehicles. Insure your trailer with a business auto insurance policy, and be sure to purchase liability, collision, uninsured motorist, and comprehensive coverage. If your volunteer is at fault in an accident, liability insurance will pay the expenses to repair the other vehicles involved in the accident. Collision insurance will pay for the damages to your trailer. If your volunteer is in an accident and is not at fault, and the other driver is not insured, uninsured motorist insurance will pay the expenses to repair your trailer. Comprehensive insurance protects you from losses that are not related to an accident. For example, acts of nature (hailstorms, floods, and falling trees), vandalism, and theft are covered by comprehensive insurance.

Typically, a volunteer's personal automobile insurance will cover your trailer, and will repair any property he damages while pulling it. Your business auto policy will cover damages to your trailer that are not covered by the volunteer's automobile insurance. For example, while pulling your trailer, if a volunteer backs the trailer into a car, his policy will repair the car. If your trailer is damaged in the process, your business auto policy will repair your trailer. Require all volunteers who pull your trailer to submit a copy of their current automobile insurance card.

Next, let's focus on your equipment, uniforms, and other property. While your business auto insurance policy covers your trailer, it will not repair or replace the contents within the trailer. Your insurance agent will most likely recommend an "inland marine" policy for "contractors' equipment (and tools) coverage." This policy will insure your uniforms, musical instruments, ATVs, and other equipment against direct physical loss.

2. **Serving concessions.** If you serve concessions as a fundraiser, you should carry general commercial liability insurance. This will protect you from a claim or lawsuit filed by a customer. For example, if you serve food that is too hot, a customer may suffer a burn. If you inadvertently serve food that has spoiled, a customer may become ill.

   Generally, coverage only applies to your customers, and does not cover student and parent volunteers. Therefore, if a student twists an ankle working a fundraiser, the student's family health insurance will cover the medical claim.

   If you serve concessions for a local university or professional sports team, they will require you to carry general liability insurance and ask to be named as an "additional insured" on the policy.

3. **Making financial transactions.** To protect your organization from embezzlement, theft, and fraud, consider carrying fidelity bond insurance. This insurance will protect the organization from losses caused by the fraudulent and dishonest acts of its volunteers.[41]

   You may be aware of an insurance product that is recommended for some nonprofits: directors and officers insurance. This protects an executive board against the liability of wrong decisions and mismanagement of funds. Since a typical booster organization does not invest funds or hire employees, the risk of being named in a lawsuit is very low. Additionally, schools are public institutions and are not subject to certain kinds of liability. Therefore, discuss your need for directors and officers insurance with your agent before writing a policy.

Do you think your organization may need additional liability coverage beyond your basic policies? If so, talk with your insurance agent about the feasibility of an umbrella policy. An umbrella policy provides coverage above and beyond the specified limits of your other policies. Additionally, it may cover losses that are not included within the other policies.[42]

In summary, you and your volunteers work too hard to allow unnecessary risks to undermine the financial health of your organization. Proactively assess your organization's risks, and then take action to reduce those risks. With the help of a trusted agent, take out insurance policies that will protect your organization's assets. Then you may move forward with confidence that your organization will be financially secure, even through the worst of events.

Leadership Essential #24: Assess the risks to your organization and carry insurance to reduce those risks.

TWENTY-TWO

Present Financial Data with Clarity

As a nonprofit, a booster organization is obligated to share its financial status with its members. Working toward a common goal, you have asked parents to make student payments and participate in fundraisers. You owe it to them to share the results of their collective efforts.

The executive team benefits when you share your financial status with your organization. First, when parents understand the organization's flow of income and expenses, they will be more likely to respond to your call to action in times of need. They will see the importance of participating in fundraisers. For each additional item they sell or event they work, they will move the needle toward achieving the organization's common fundraising goal. Use financial status reports as a motivational tool to bring everyone together toward a common goal.

Next, sharing financial status with your organization brings accountability to the executive team. The organization's members elected you to lead with integrity. As we saw in chapter sixteen, when many people have visibility to the organization's financial status, you lower the risk of embezzlement.

You may be concerned about sharing your financial status if you are achieving your goals but not everyone is participating. What if parents who aren't contributing see that the organization is getting by without their help? Will they be prone not to contribute at all? Well, maybe. And while you do have a valid point, you should first be thankful that you are achieving your financial goals. Remember, the essence of the nonprofit is that everyone works toward a common goal and all participants receive equal benefit, regardless of their individual contribution or participation in fundraising activities. As a leader, you must come to realize that there will be some parents who simply will not contribute.

Communicate With Clarity

Whether you use graphs, charts, or tables to communicate financial status, the message must be clear and easy to understand. Readers must not only *comprehend* the message, they must also *interpret* the results correctly. Their interpretation is what will lead them into action.

Every sporting event has a scoreboard. The scoreboard immediately tells if you are winning or losing, the margin by which you are winning or losing, and the time remaining in the competition. The scoreboard motivates the team to persevere toward victory. When you effectively communicate financial status to your organization, you provide them a scoreboard. Here are six pointers to effectively communicate your financial status:

1. **Show where you're going and when you expect to get there.** Here's a rule of thumb for communicating progress toward a goal: *From X to Y by when.* X is your starting point and Y is your ending point, your goal. Be sure to indicate by when,

meaning the date that you expect to achieve your goal.

2. **Make it easy to tell if you are winning.** Where are you now? Where should you be? When communicated effectively, this should be intuitive to your reader.

3. **Include a target.** The target shows where you should be at any given point in time. On a graph, the target is best shown as a line.

4. **Use color for added clarity.** Use these universally recognized colors to reflect your status:

   • **Green.** You're at or above the target
   • **Yellow.** You're close but not achieving the target
   • **Red.** You're under the target.

   For example, in a bar graph, color the bar appropriately to emphasize the status.

5. **Add an icon.** For added clarity, include an icon, such as a happy (or sad) face, a thumbs up (or down), or a traffic light. Be creative, and add an icon that your audience will immediately connect with.

6. **Publicize your status.** Once you have prepared your graph, chart, or table, communicate it through as many channels as possible. Be sure to report your financial status in booster meetings, in monthly newsletters, and on your website.

Communicate the Right Information at the Right Time

Now that we've seen how to communicate your financial status with clarity, let's consider what and when to communicate. Here are five important financial indicators to report to your members:

1. **Progress toward projected income.** This is best shown by a bar graph, reflecting progress toward the actual income required to run the organization (not including pass-through funds – see chapter seventeen). Report your progress monthly.

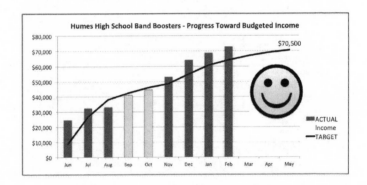

2. **Monthly cash flow.** A table shows this best. Include your starting bank account balance, all income received, all expenses paid, and the ending bank account balance. The monthly financial report that I showed you in chapter sixteen is a good template to report monthly cash flow.

3. **Progress toward a fundraising goal.** This can be shown in a bar or line graph, or a "thermometer" chart. Use your illustration to motivate your

students and parents toward higher levels of participation. During a fundraising campaign, report your progress as frequently as possible to sustain momentum. Here's an example from the Blaze Band Boosters.

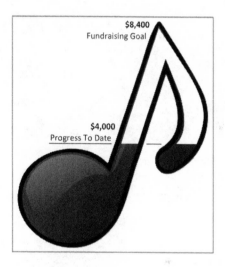

4. **End of year reflection.** A pie chart allows you to visually divide something into its individual parts and to show each part's proportion to the whole. Income, expenses, and many other financial indicators may be represented by a pie chart. Since a pie chart depicts a snapshot in time, it lends itself well to an end of year reflection.

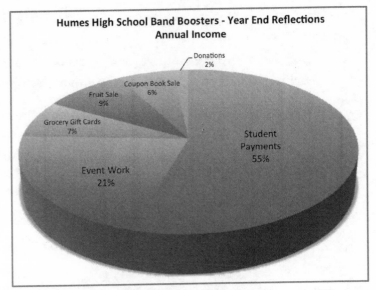

Humes High School Band Boosters - Year End Reflections
Annual Income

Donations 2%
Coupon Book Sale 6%
Fruit Sale 9%
Grocery Gift Cards 7%
Event Work 21%
Student Payments 55%

5. **Progress toward a major or multi-year capital campaign goal.** A "thermometer" chart is a great tool to reflect progress toward a major capital campaign goal. Establish milestone dates when you will update your "thermometer," then create a strategy to achieve each milestone.

In this chapter, we've learned that a booster organization is obligated to share its financial status with its members. We've seen six best practices to communicate financial status with clarity. Whether you use a graph, chart, or table, your financial report is your scoreboard, and members should immediately know if the organization is winning or losing.

Remember the five important financial indicators to report to your members: progress toward projected income, monthly cash flow, progress toward a fundraising goal, an end-of-year reflection, and progress toward a major or multi-year campaign goal. Reporting the status of these indicators will help you keep everyone working toward common financial goals.

Leadership Essential #25: Communicate financial status clearly and in a timely manner.

PART FOUR

THE COMMUNICATIONS
LEADER

TWENTY-THREE

Recruit Effective Communicators

When it comes to communication, we live in an unprecedented time. Never before have there been so many media outlets vying for our attention. Today's media "noise" has created a distracted audience that has little tolerance for lengthy and unclear messages.

This environment creates significant implications for your booster organization as well. When communicating internally, you must be clear, to the point, and right on time or else your members will ignore you. When communicating externally, you've got to compete with other extracurricular programs in your school and community just to be heard. Therefore, well-written communications are vital to your organization's livelihood.

There are a variety of communication roles within a booster organization. Five examples are shown below. Effective communicators are hard to come by. If you do not have enough qualified volunteers to fill every role, be sure to cover the major tasks with the people you have.

1. **Secretary.** The secretary records and maintains minutes of booster and executive team meetings, announces upcoming events, and manages the membership roster. The secretary is traditionally an elected officer and executive team member.

2. **Newsletter Committee chair.** The newsletter chair compiles and publishes the organization's

newsletter. Additional volunteers may help with the printing and distribution of a hardcopy newsletter.

3. **Publicity Committee chair.** The publicity chair promotes the extracurricular program to an external audience within the school and community. The publicity chair is always looking for ways to advance the program, through traditional media outlets, such as newspaper and television, and through modern social media channels.

4. **Webmaster or administrator.** The webmaster maintains the organization's on-line content. The key to success in this role is to post accurate and timely content.

5. **Historian.** The historian keeps a record of milestone events that collectively tell the program's story.

In the next few chapters, we'll discuss specific types of communications. But first, let's take a look at the attributes of an effective communications leader.

1. **Exceptional written communication skills.** An effective written communicator is proficient in spelling and grammar. His writing is clear and succinct, represents the organization professionally and positively, and appeals to a wide audience.

2. **Attention to detail.** The majority of your communications will have a specific call to action. An effective communicator creates thorough and accurate messages, and ensures that all relevant information is passed along.

3. **Competent in the use of electronic technology.** In this digital age, competency with

word processing software and the ability to publish in PDF format is a must. Additionally, an effective electronic communicator understands email basics and is capable of managing multiple distribution lists. She also navigates websites and uploads and downloads files and data.

4. **Thorough understanding of the organization's activities.** This is really a prerequisite. Some of the best communications stem from personal experience. Therefore, an effective communications leader participates in all of the organization's major activities and encourages others to participate as well.

5. **Enthusiasm for the extracurricular program.** Enthusiasm for the extracurricular program provides a solid foundation for captivating internal and external communications.

6. **Interpersonal skills.** An effective communications leader collaborates with parents and the executive team to help accomplish the organization's goals. She quickly resolves conflicts and works to prevent factions and cliques from forming.

7. **Organizational skills.** Your communications' timing is as important as its content. You need a leader who plans and organizes his work for maximum productivity and efficiency. An effective planner brings order to situations, solves problems, and eliminates chaos.

8. **Self-starting mindset.** Seek out a communications leader who is disciplined and

driven to follow plans through completion. A self-starter takes initiative and seldom has to be reminded to complete assigned tasks.

9. **Commitment to attend all meetings.** A dedicated communications leader makes meeting attendance a priority. She is trustworthy and follows through on her obligation to attend meetings and perform all duties of the role.

A thriving booster organization understands the impact of compelling communications. We have examined communications roles, and we have seen the attributes for success. Above all, your communications leader must produce content that is clear, concise, and timely for your organization to be heard in a noisy world.

Leadership Essential #26: Compelling internal and external communications are vital to an organization's livelihood.

TWENTY-FOUR

Spread the Word

Would you like to boost attendance at your monthly meetings and other events? The most effective method I've found is to send clear, concise, and timely personal reminders. Parents' schedules can be overwhelming at times, with many priorities competing for their time. Even the most faithful, trustworthy core group of parents needs a gentle reminder every now and then.

So what is a "personal" reminder? Is it a message specifically crafted for each individual? No, it is a common message delivered to each parent in your organization by email or voice mail. You may post upcoming events on your website and newsletter calendars, but that is simply not enough. Social media is a good supplement, but not as effective as the personal message. From my experience, many parents are not early adopters into the latest technology. However, most parents have become conditioned to check their email and voice mail boxes.

The mere act of sending personal reminders doesn't guarantee that you will boost attendance at your meetings and events. You must carefully construct your message to drive participation. Here are five easy steps to help you develop more effective messages:

1. **Start with a meaningful subject line.** When communicating by email, summarize your core message in the subject line. Capture your readers' attention and give them a reason to open the

message. Let's create an example subject line for an upcoming booster meeting.

REMINDER: Blaze Band Booster Meeting – Tuesday @ 7:00 PM

We caught the readers' attention with the word "REMINDER" in all caps, and then identified the upcoming meeting, day, and time. Even if readers don't open the message, at least they will know the upcoming booster meeting is scheduled for Tuesday at 7 o'clock.

2. **Clearly state your call to action.** What do you want your readers to do in response to your message? To have them act upon your request, create a clear and concise call to action statement. After reading your call to action, readers should know exactly what you are asking of them.

A banner statement across the top of the email is an effective way to call the reader to action. Format this statement in bold italics, and center it above the body of the message. Here's the call to action for our upcoming booster meeting:

Please Plan to Attend the Blaze Band Booster Meeting
Tuesday April 9th, 7:00 PM

3. **Keep it brief and to the point.** In this digital age, people receive many messages throughout the day. If they open your email to find a long message that

looks too dense, they are likely to give up and move on. Likewise, when using a voice messaging service, people will likely hang up if your message rambles on and on.

Use simple, easy to understand words and keep your sentences short. Don't use jargon or acronyms that some people may not understand. Here's the body text for our upcoming booster meeting:

> Please plan to join us Tuesday evening for a time of reflection and fun as we bring the school year to a close. I'll share a presentation of booster accomplishments from the past few years. We'll also reveal the Blaze Band survey results!

4. **Generate suspense with a "hook."** A "teaser" in the body of your message will generate readers' interest and give them an incentive to attend your event. In our example, we included the "hook," *"We'll also reveal the Blaze Band survey results!"* Leading up to this meeting, parents and students had been encouraged to contribute their favorite memories and experiences through an on-line survey. Survey results will be shared for the first time during this booster meeting.

5. **Proofread what you have written, and read it aloud.** Proofreading your work may seem elementary to some, but I often receive messages that obviously have not been proofread or screened. This essential step in the communication process will help ensure that your message will be clearly

understood. For an added check, read your draft out loud. You'll be amazed how this technique will expose an awkward cadence that you cannot detect by reading silently.

Here's our full message, complete with greeting and closing:

From: Blackman Band Boosters <blackmanbandboosters@example.com>
To:
Sunday, April 7, 2013 4:50 PM
REMINDER: Blaze Band Booster Meeting - Tuesday @ 7:00 PM

Please Plan to Attend the Blaze Band Booster Meeting
Tuesday April 9th, 7:00 PM

Hello Blaze Band Booster families and students!

Please plan to join us Tuesday evening for a time of reflection and fun as we bring the school year to a close. I'll share a presentation of booster accomplishments from the past few years. We'll also reveal the Blaze Band survey results!

I hope to see you Tuesday at 7:00!

Dan Caldwell, President
Blaze Band Boosters

Now that you have developed a meaningful message, it's time to focus on the delivery of your message. Here are four tips that will improve the impact of your personal reminders:

1. **Carefully select an electronic messaging provider.** Every booster organization should have its own email provider and, if you choose, voice message service. Establish a dedicated email address as a window for all of your communications. This will represent your organization in a professional manner, as opposed to channeling communications through someone's personal email. It will also provide consistency as leaders transition into and

out of their roles from year to year. Here are four considerations to help you identify appropriate messaging providers:

- **Easy to use.** Choose a service that is easy for you to administrate and provides a user-friendly interface for your parents. Your email service should facilitate two-way communication between you and your parents. Look for features such as message forwarding. This service allows you to automatically forward email to another address that you check more frequently.

- **Will not kick your email to the recipients' spam folders.** Choose a well-known and respected email service to minimize the chance of your emails ending up in your members' spam folders. You should also encourage your members to add your organization's email address to their contact lists. Finally, send an occasional trial email to selected recipients to detect if your message routes to spam.

- **Cost effective.** The email service provider industry is highly competitive, and many reputable services are free. From my personal experience in a program with more than 200 students, Google's Gmail[43] and Yahoo! Mail[44] provide great service and are free to use. One Call Now[45] provides an easy to use, automated voice message service at a reasonable rate.

- **Accommodates distribution lists.** Distribution lists are the single most effective organizational tools to manage your electronic communications. Find a provider that not only supports distribution lists, but also accommodates the number of participants in your program. Most free providers limit the number of recipients per message or the total number of messages sent per day. Before establishing service, check your headcount to be sure you'll be okay.

2. **Create separate distribution lists for each grade level.** As students come into and graduate out of the program, grade level distribution lists will help you ensure that you're communicating with the right people. Grade level distribution lists allow you to remove all graduating seniors with one command. A best practice is to name each list by graduating class, for example, "Class of 20xx." Over the long run, this will be much easier than naming each list "freshman, sophomore, junior, and senior" because you'll never have to change the lists' names.

3. **Schedule the publication of your messages.** Never send a reminder more than one week in advance. If you do, someone will inevitably misread the reminder and show up on the corresponding day a week (or more) early. Issue your first reminder six days in advance, then send a follow-up reminder two days prior to the event. For example, if your booster meeting is on Tuesday, send your first reminder the prior Wednesday, then follow up with a second reminder on Sunday. Avoid sending reminders the day before, because some people don't check their email that often. Also, never send a reminder the

day of an event. This reflects poor organizational skills on behalf of booster leadership, and it is inconsiderate of your parents' time.

4. **Don't underestimate the power of the personal reminder.** Never miss an opportunity to promote your events. Reminders really do work. Once, our secretary forgot to issue a reminder for a booster meeting and that resulted in the lowest attendance during my tenure with the organization. Many of our faithful volunteers apologized for missing the meeting, and let me know how much they rely on a simple meeting reminder to stay on track.

In summary, the most effective method to increase attendance at your booster events is to send reminder messages. Email and voice messages tend to have the highest response rates. The most effective messages are clear, concise, and sent in a timely manner. When you are intentional and strategic in advertising your events, you will enjoy the highest possible attendance and participation.

Leadership Essential #27: Clear, concise, and timely reminders will increase attendance and participation in your organization's events.

TWENTY-FIVE

Document Your Meetings

Keeping minutes is one of the most important and often overlooked tasks in a booster organization. Many organizations simply fail to record the decisions and assignments they make during their meetings. This is often because people are reluctant to volunteer due to the complexity of the minutes format, the perceived time requirement, and a lack of confidence in their writing skills. The good news is there is a quick and easy way to document your meetings. We'll examine that later; but first, let's consider why minutes are important. Here are five reasons your organization should keep meeting minutes:

1. **To record the decisions made during the meeting.** Without documentation, decisions are subject to individuals' interpretation and recollection. Among legal circles, there is a common understanding that if it's not in the minutes, it didn't happen.

   Minutes should not only capture decisions, but also the important details that accompany them. For example, if a decision is made to purchase an item, a maximum purchase price, preferred vendor, and person responsible for making the purchase should also be specified.

2. **To record who participated in the meeting.** It is important to know who the decision makers were in the meeting. There are times when it is equally as

important to know who was absent when decisions were made.

3. **To record assigned tasks, responsible people, and due dates.** This provides a clear understanding of the task, not only for the assignee, but also for everyone involved. When a task is assigned and documented, there is an additional level of accountability for it to be done.

4. **To provide an official record of elections.** The minutes that document your elections authorize your officers to conduct financial business for the organization. Your banker will not authorize people to sign checks on the booster account without a copy of these minutes. You may also have to provide a copy with your annual IRS tax return.

5. **To show accountability to parents and school administrators.** Your repository of meeting minutes show your parents and school administrators that you are operating with integrity and transparency. Executive team minutes provide evidence that you are operating in good faith, by sound procedures, and in compliance with tax law.

Now that we have seen and understand the reasons why minutes are important to a booster organization, let's look at how to effectively keep them. Unless you are specifically required to follow the Robert's Rules of Order format for meeting minutes, try a more streamlined approach. Meeting minutes do not have to provide a transcript of the meeting. If people want that much detail, they should attend the meeting! Below are the six important attributes to capture in your meeting minutes. You can see how they all come together in the example minutes at the end of the chapter.

1. **Date, time, and location.** Recurring meetings are usually held at the same time and in the same location, so pre-load that information into your minutes template. Generally, the only information that will change is the meeting date.

2. **Presiding officer, scribe, and participants.** For executive team meetings, pre-load the team members' names into the template. When documenting each meeting, show participation by making the attendees' names bold. For booster meeting minutes, a simple note that a quorum had been reached will suffice.

3. **Agenda.** Copy and paste the agenda from your pre-meeting email into the minutes template.

   Before we move on, take note of how easy it has been to record the meeting information.

4. **Decisions and agreements.** Remember to include all of the background information that accompanies each decision. The goal is to be clear so that each decision will be interpreted exactly as it was agreed upon during the meeting.

5. **Action items.** Describe the tasks that are to be done along with the responsible people and due dates. Before the meeting adjourns, be sure that everyone understands his or her assigned tasks and due dates.

6. **Meeting notes.** This section is not intended to be a transcript of all that was said. Rather, it should reflect only the most important discussion points

that aren't necessarily a decision or action item. The example minutes at the end of the chapter will give you a feel for the type of information to include as meeting notes.

There are two additional considerations when documenting minutes. First, be prompt. A best practice is to send a draft to the team within 24 hours of the meeting. This allows the team to report any differences in their understanding while the meeting is still fresh on their minds. It also adds emphasis for assignees to promptly complete their time-sensitive tasks.

Next, save and distribute minutes in PDF format. Nearly every computer has a PDF reader. For those that do not, free PDF software is available for download. This is important for two reasons. First, a PDF maintains the document's original format. It is not likely to be distorted if the reader's format settings are different than yours. Second, it is not easily changed. While it is not likely that a recipient would intentionally change your minutes, someone could inadvertently delete a section by mistake.

As we have seen, it is critical for a booster organization to keep adequate records of their meetings. The complex format and rigor required to document traditional minutes is somewhat intimidating, but it doesn't have to be. Using a streamlined template, vital booster information may be documented efficiently and accurately.

Leadership Essential #28: A booster organization that operates with integrity maintains accurate meeting minutes.

The Booster Leader

Humes High School Band Boosters – Executive Team Meeting

Meeting Information

Date & Time	Location	Presiding
November 13, 2012	6:15 p.m.	CHS Room 105	Fred Griggs (president)

Agenda	Scribe
1. Fruit sale – plan for distribution – Thanksgiving and Christmas (exam week) deliveries	Lisa Edwards (secretary)
	Participants (attendees indicated in bold)
2. Annual Trip	**Ron Miller** (vice president)
a. Schedule a 10-day out meeting for Mr. Roberts to speak to parents – target Tuesday 2/5/13	**Melanie Carr** (treasurer)
	Audrey Black (bookkeeper)
b. Chaperone, room, and bus assignment process	**Cathy Perkins** (instructor)
3. Banquet – preliminary planning	**Brad Franklin** (instructor)
4. 2013~2014 funding	Amanda Perry (finance chair)
a. Determine fundraising activities	
b. Establish amount for student payment	
c. Schedule a meeting for parent participation	
5. Review financials and performance to budget	

Decisions & Agreements

1. The annual trip 10-day out "what to expect" meeting for parents and students will be Tuesday, February 5, 2013, assuming Mr. Roberts' (Superior Tours) availability.
2. 2013~2014 financial planning will be included as an agenda item during the February 5th booster meeting.

Action Items

	Task	Date Due	Assigned To
1.	Invite Mr. Roberts (Superior Tours) to the 10-day out trip preparation meeting on February 5th.	November 19th	Fred Griggs
2.	Update the website to include the new booster meeting of February 5th.	Upon confirmation of Mr. Roberts' availability	Brad Franklin
3.	Annual trip – create chaperone & bus assignment lists (with help from instructors and Fred).	January 15th	Amanda Perry
4.	Contact Expo Hall to begin the process of reserving space for the spring banquet. Target banquet date Monday, May 6th.	November 19th	Fred Griggs
5.	Develop a note to attach to blank checks as they are distributed, requiring the checks to be spent or returned within seven days.	January 15th	Melanie Carr

Meeting Notes

- Thanksgiving fruit will be delivered to the school at 8:00 a.m. Friday November 16th. The instructors will recruit student labor to help unload the truck. Students will be instructed to have all fruit picked-up by 4:00 p.m.
- 2013~2014 fundraising:
  - Fruit sale – consider requesting each student to sell fruit or pay an equivalent amount (of profit) to the boosters.
  - Potential fundraiser – Brad Franklin will investigate the potential to conduct a raffle. Specifically, what permission do the county school board and Secretary of State's office require? This option will be presented during the financial planning section of the February 5th booster meeting.
- Financial reports for the month of October were reviewed and approved, and are attached with the distribution of the minutes.

TWENTY-SIX

Deliver the News

Does your organization publish a newsletter? If so, are you getting the maximum benefit from it? A newsletter can contribute tremendous value to an organization. Your parents are in a season of life where many priorities compete for their time. A newsletter helps keep your organization top of mind. Here are seven reasons your organization should publish a newsletter:

1. **To stay in contact with your parents.** A newsletter provides the opportunity to reach every member of the organization on a frequent basis. Generally, only a core group of members attend booster meetings, so a newsletter helps build a sense of community among all members.

2. **To let the parents hear from the instructor.** Instructors interact with students on a daily basis, but may rarely see the parents. An instructor's message will let parents get to know the instructor on a more personal level.

3. **To let the parents hear from the booster president.** Many parents only attend the major booster events. Therefore, the primary message they hear is a request for funding and participation. A newsletter column lets the booster president connect with the parents without the hard sell for their support. I used the president's message as an opportunity to encourage the students and parents.

The most popular was a series of messages based upon inspirational quotes from musicians and well-respected people. Along with each quote, I wrote a couple of paragraphs applying the theme to our band program and organization.

4. **To let the parents hear from a student leader.** Parents love to hear how students benefit from the program. Student testimonials provide a "return on investment" for the parents' time, effort, and funding. Be creative. Ask your students to write guest posts or have your newsletter editor interview students.

5. **To provide a long-range calendar.** Give your parents advance notice of booster events so that they can block the time on their personal calendars. Include at least three months of events in each newsletter's calendar.

6. **To show monthly progress toward achieving your annual income goal.** In chapter twenty-two, we learned how to effectively communicate progress toward financial initiatives. A graph showing your progress will help keep everyone engaged in fundraising activities and "moving the needle" to achieve the overall goal.

7. **To announce upcoming events.** Don't assume that word will travel home with students. Use your newsletter to announce upcoming meetings and fundraising events. Be sure to include the "who, what, when, and where" so that everyone will clearly understand what you're asking them to do.

These seven points illustrate the value that newsletters can add to an organization. Now let's consider how to deliver the most impact with every newsletter. Here are seven best practices for effective newsletters:

1. **Provide meaningful content.** Make your newsletters pertinent and valuable to your parents. Go beyond simply communicating facts. Encourage your instructor, president, and contributing students to tell stories that will compel the reader to participate and support the organization.

2. **Make it personal.** Rather than making broad announcements to the masses, write as if you are having a conversation with one person. After all, only one person will read the newsletter at a time. This subtle change in style will dramatically improve the effectiveness of your message. Instead of, "We are asking that everyone sell four boxes of fruit," write, "We ask you to sell four boxes of fruit." This is much more personal, clear, and concise. Additionally, many times when a message goes out to "everyone," "no one" actually answers the call.

3. **Include specific calls to action in the headlines.** If your parents only read the headlines, will they know what you want them to do? Build calls to action into your headlines, and provide supporting details within your articles. Make it easy for your parents to follow up and take the action you desire.

4. **Make it easy to read.** People are turned off by very dense text on a page. Many times they will not even attempt to read something that appears to be

long and complex. Keep your sentences and paragraphs short. As a rule of thumb, limit your sentences to around fifteen words and your paragraphs to about three sentences.

5. **Choose a visually appealing template.** Continuing the mindset of making your newsletter easy to read, select a template that is clean and uncluttered. There are many free newsletter templates included with Microsoft Word and Apple Pages. Microsoft's Office.com[46] website gives you even more free newsletter templates to choose from. Another option is to create a custom newsletter in Microsoft PowerPoint or Apple Keynote. You can even create a newsletter on an iPad with the Pages app.

Choose a font that is pleasing to the eye, and use it consistently throughout your newsletter. A newsletter with several different font styles is visually confusing. Additionally, maintain a consistent font size. Ten point or greater will keep your text from becoming too dense and difficult to read.

6. **Publish your newsletter regularly.** In chapter nine, we developed an annual plan for the organization, including newsletter publication and distribution dates. Be intentional to meet each month's publication date. In addition to keeping booster activities top of mind, you can use it as a reminder for upcoming booster meetings. In the Blaze Band Boosters, we distributed newsletters to

arrive in homes on Friday or Saturday prior to our booster meeting on Tuesday night.

7. **Distribute your newsletter through many channels.** Be sure to take advantage of all the new and innovative media to deliver your newsletter. In addition to the U.S. Mail, post your newsletter on your website and Facebook page, and tweet the link to your followers. As we saw in chapter twenty-five, remember to save and distribute your newsletter in PDF format.

A newsletter allows you to connect with your parents on a frequent basis, provide a personal touch, and keep everyone focused toward achieving financial goals. With minimal effort, you can create and publish impactful newsletters that benefit your organization.

Leadership Essential #29: A thriving booster organization publishes impactful newsletters on a consistent basis.

TWENTY-SEVEN

Engage Your Organization with Social Media

The digital age has changed the way we work, shop, and interact with others. Social media has brought new meaning to the familiar terms, "friend," "like," and "viral." Many of your parents already use social media, and its use will only increase as future generations of parents who are already accustomed to it rotate into your organization. Social media provides the conduit for a booster organization to engage its members. Its interactive nature allows users to join in the conversation. Through social media, extended family in other towns may join the booster community.

Let's look at how the major types of social media can impact your booster organization.

Microblogging

Social media researchers Andreas Kaplan and Michael Haenlein define a microblog as an internet based application "which allows users to exchange small elements of content such as short sentences, individual images, or video links."[47] Twitter is the most popular microblog, enabling "users to send and read 'tweets,' which are text messages limited to 140 characters"[48] (Wikipedia). One of Twitter's major benefits is that it is mobile. You can reach your parents wherever they are at almost any time of day. Twitter is easy to set up, and it is even easier for your parents to follow you. Best of all, if they retweet your messages, you will reach a much broader audience including their followers.

Here are a few ideas for tweets:

- Practice and rehearsal call times
- Scores and contest updates
- Travel updates from the road
- Announcements and reminders
- Links to newsletters and other important documents
- Photos and short videos from practices and events

Media Sharing

Media sharing sites allow users to upload photos, videos, and audio to a website that can be accessed from anywhere in the world.[49] YouTube is the most popular video-sharing site, allowing users to upload, view, and share videos for free.[50] YouTube expands your organization's reach, allowing people in faraway places to see your games, performances, and practices. You can even create a dedicated YouTube channel for all of your organization's videos. Consumers of your content may subscribe to your channel and choose to be alerted by email when you upload something new. YouTube makes it easier than ever to bring out-of-town relatives into your community. When you engage extended families and they see the value your program brings to the students, they are more likely to support you with a financial contribution.

Here are a few ideas for videos to share:

- Highlights from games, performances, and practices
- Major booster meetings, such as the annual kick-off meeting

- Special announcements from the instructor or a selected booster officer
- Promotional video, perhaps prepared by the students

Social Networking

Social networking sites facilitate building a community of people who "share interests, activities, backgrounds, or real-life connections."[51] Facebook is currently the largest social networking site, with 1.11 billion people using the site each month.[52] Interactivity makes Facebook the most powerful form of social media to promote your organization. Users may comment on, "like," and share your content with other users.

You can use Facebook to communicate practically anything, from announcements, reminders, and calendars to photos and videos. Beware of a common pitfall, though – inactivity. Your audience will expect to see new content on a regular basis. If they don't, they'll lose interest and fall away. Seek out a "power user" to maintain your organization's presence on Facebook.

Social Media's Impact on a Booster Organization

A local radio station's contest opened my eyes to the power of social media. In the contest, high school music programs were invited to compete for a $5000 donation. Each school uploaded a video of a performance to YouTube, and all the schools' videos were linked to the radio station's website. Over a two-week period, fans visited the site to vote for their favorite performance. Fans commented on Facebook, and the station displayed the comments on their website.

The radio station did not publish a leader board through the course of the contest, so we never knew where we stood in the vote count. However, I made a couple of discoveries by analyzing social media data. First, the number of YouTube views measured each program's external appeal to all voters. Voting was not linked to video views, so anyone could watch a competitor's video without casting a vote for that competitor. Therefore, the most compelling videos pulled in the highest number of views.

Next, Facebook comments and "likes" measured each program's internal support from their own fan base. People would comment on and "like" their own program's video, but no one would "like" a competitor's video.

When I examined the data, I compared both measures, external (YouTube views) and internal (Facebook comments and "likes"). The results were intriguing. Many programs with a captivating performance and high YouTube views did not garner internal fan support through Facebook comments and "likes." Similarly, several programs with high internal support lacked the overall appeal to drive YouTube views.

I plotted these two measures on a graph (shown at the end of the chapter). The very best performance in each category, external and internal, would land a school in the upper right quadrant of the graph. I was very pleased to see that the Blaze Band ranked #1 in my unofficial social media analysis.

In the end, we did not win the $5000 donation – it went to a very deserving rural school. However, social media helped to engage our members and generate a great deal of publicity for our program.

Social media is here to stay. In this chapter, we have seen the impact that the three major types of social media, microblogging (Twitter), media sharing (YouTube), and social networking (Facebook) have on an organization. It is not difficult for an organization to participate in social media, but it does require a commitment to maintain a presence on-line. Seek out a competent, self-starting volunteer to lead the organization's social media strategy.

Leadership Essential #30: Use social media to engage your organization's members.

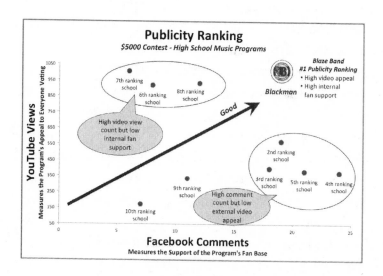

TWENTY-EIGHT

Build Your Brand

What is your program's reputation within the school and community? How do outsiders view your booster organization? What is the first thing that pops into people's minds when they hear your program's name? Whether you realize it or not, every program and booster organization has its own "brand."

Your brand is comprised of people's perceptions, whether they reflect reality or not. People's perceptions are molded one encounter at a time. For example, do your fans welcome the opposing team and fans, or subject them to boos and other rude acts? When your booster volunteers work concessions, do they greet customers with a friendly welcome and thank them for their support?

It takes many positive experiences to establish a positive brand image, and only a few negative experiences to diminish it. The missteps of an instructor, parent, or student can tarnish a program's or organization's reputation. Therefore, a booster organization can benefit its program by overseeing and intentionally building the brand.

The Importance of a Strong Brand

One of an extracurricular program's greatest attributes is respect within the school and community. Here are four benefits that a strong brand contributes to a program and booster organization:

1. **A strong brand communicates the program's image.** Every sporting program wants to be known by its winning record and championships. Fine arts programs desire to provide entertaining performances. They also want their students to achieve in district and regional competitions. All extracurricular programs want their graduates to excel at the collegiate level.

   A booster organization should not only publicize these student achievements, but also promote the organization's core values. Respect and integrity should be at the top of the list, and other important attributes should be communicated as well. How do you want your program to be perceived? Is it innovative and cool? Welcoming and inclusive? Character building? Decide upon the most important attributes and develop a strategy to promote those attributes within the school and community.

2. **A strong brand creates a value proposition.** "A value proposition is a promise of value to be delivered and a belief from the customer that value will be experienced."[53] (Wikipedia). You want your extracurricular program to be a destination that parents will guide their children toward. A strong brand is one of the best recruiting tools you can have because students (and their parents) are drawn to a vibrant program.

Some states now require students to choose an elective path of focus. For example, the Tennessee Department of Education recently modified its graduation requirements to better prepare students for college.[54] The core curriculum leaves little room for electives, and students must select a three-year continuous elective path. Therefore, fine arts programs (band, choir, etc.) are pitted against other option paths such as career and technical, math and science, humanities, advanced placement, and international baccalaureate. Fine arts programs now face competition from other electives like never before. A meaningful value proposition will set your program apart and lure prospective students from the competition.

3. **A strong brand fills the pipeline with parent volunteers.** A solid value proposition will not only attract new students to your program, it will attract their parents too. Many parents want to participate in this stage of their children's lives. It is important to let them know that there is a place for them to fit in, and that the parents have fun too!

4. **A strong brand generates "buzz" about the program.** In marketing circles, "buzz" is a term that represents what others are saying about you. When properly focused, it is free advertisement and promotion for your program. Buzz is much more valuable to a program than a similar method of promotion – hype. Hype is what you are saying about yourself. Work diligently to create a positive

message about your program that people will want to spread to one another.

How You Can Build Your Brand

Now that we've seen the benefits, let's look at a few ways to create a strong brand.

1. **Create a publicity committee.** Assemble a small team of volunteers to develop and execute a promotional strategy within the school and community. Seek out parents for this committee who work in the field of marketing or who have connections with local media outlets.

2. **Develop a tagline or slogan.** This tagline should generate excitement for your program in just a few words. For example, we created the tagline, *"Blaze Band: Feel the Fire!"* Incorporate the tagline into all of your program's promotions and advertising.

3. **Invite the news media to cover your events.** Invite the news media to cover practices, banquets, and other special events. If you sponsor a sporting team, pitch stories to the media that go beyond the typical game coverage. Create an opportunity to showcase the students' character and personalities while promoting your program.

   Occasionally, you'll have a student who has overcome incredible challenges to accomplish extraordinary things. Michael Stanaland is a percussionist in the Blaze Band and an inspiration to his classmates. Michael was born with cerebral palsy and gets around in a wheelchair. In order to fulfill his dream of marching in the football band, his mother Renae learned the drill and pushes his wheelchair in the halftime show. One of our parents reached out to the local media, and his story ran in the newspaper[55] and on television.[56] Michael was very happy that the publicity promoted his band program.

4. **Maintain a presence on social media.** In the last chapter, we saw how social media can engage an organization to work toward a common goal. To make the most of this media channel, be sure that your content is meaningful and useful. Don't post too frequently, which may overwhelm and keep people from joining the conversation. Likewise, don't let too much time pass between posts and allow them to lose interest. You may have to test this a bit to determine what your members prefer.

5. **Invite your school board member to a booster meeting.** Without booster organization sponsorship, most school boards would not be able to offer extracurricular activities. Reach out and invite the school board member who represents your zone to a booster meeting. You'll benefit in two ways. First, your school board member will have the opportunity to see your operation first hand. Second, your parents will have the opportunity to meet her face to face. At times, school boards and booster organizations may not see things eye to eye. Therefore, when you can meet and talk on a personal level, both parties will have a better understanding of the other's circumstances.

6. **Establish relationships with your booster counterparts in the community.** Take the opportunity to get to know the leaders in booster organizations at other schools. After all, they share the same goal as you – to provide an outstanding extracurricular experience for the students. Don't get caught up in competition; let the students take care of that on the field or court. Rather, find common ground and work together to realize synergies. Share best practices with each other. By taking the first step to establish relationships with your counterparts, you will create a level of trust and respect that will build your organization's brand and reputation.

Midway through my term as president, I met with my counterparts from the other band programs in town to share best practices. A couple of weeks after our meeting, one of the bands was in a bus accident on the way to a marching competition. Fortunately everyone in the band was okay, but the bus driver suffered broken bones and the driver of the other car died at the scene. Since I personally knew my fellow booster president, the tragedy had a much deeper impact, and I was better prepared to reach out and offer our support.

7. **Participate in a community service project.** Extracurricular activities build character on and off the field. Sometimes it is good to take a step back and put things into perspective. Work with your instructor to schedule a community service project for your program. You will build your brand by

creating goodwill in the community, and your students will learn a valuable life lesson about helping others in the process.

8. **Post an "about" page to your website.** If you don't already have an "about" page for your booster organization, create one. If you do, take a look at the message you convey. Be authentic and transparent, friendly and inviting. Post a message that will spark enthusiasm for your program and encourage new parents to get involved.

Whether you realize it or not, all programs have their own brand. When properly managed, you can reap the rewards of a strong brand. A strong brand casts a favorable image of the program and organization within the school and community. Along with this image comes a value proposition that attracts new students and their parents. With a strong brand, you'll have people talking, generating buzz for your program.

There are several ways to build your brand. The overarching premise, though, is to simply make it a priority. Establish a publicity committee to develop a strategy to promote your program. Then be intentional in executing your strategy.

Leadership Essential #31: Develop and execute a strategy to promote and build the brand of your program.

PART FIVE

THE COMMITTEE
LEADER

TWENTY-NINE

Empower Committees to Succeed

When I became the Blaze Band Boosters' president, I was immediately faced with a predicament that led to one of the greatest success stories during my tenure. Over the prior couple of years, our Truck & Equipment Committee had dwindled to only two adult volunteers – parents of graduating seniors – and a hand full of students. The adult volunteers pulled our two equipment trailers to football games and events. At the end of each school year, the band performs at the graduation ceremony, which is held at our local university across town. Graduation is a transition point for the band, and since both volunteers had graduating seniors, no one was left to move our equipment. After several phone calls and some creative alternate planning, I was able to arrange transportation of our equipment to the graduation ceremony (seemingly without a day to spare).

The urgency of this predicament really drove home the importance of succession planning within the organization. While the two prior volunteers met the need for transportation at the moment, they didn't welcome new volunteers into the crew and failed to sustain the committee's activities into the future. They also put the band at risk. If either of them had an illness, mechanical trouble, or even a scheduling conflict, there would not have been an alternate driver to take his place. While some committees' tasks are flexible and easily altered, the band simply does not travel without a fully functioning truck & equipment committee.

Using the best practices of recruiting, I set out to find a Truck & Equipment Committee chair for the upcoming school year. I spoke to a lot of people, but didn't use the hard sell. The role was just too important to put in the wrong person's hands. The time I invested in the recruiting process paid huge dividends when Steve agreed to fill the role.

Steve was a great leader and created a culture of acceptance. Under his leadership, the committee grew to more than twenty adult volunteers. Steve was so good at planning and delegating that he rarely lifted a piece of equipment himself. He was also humble enough that it bothered him not to jump in and help. However, he didn't want to deny any of his volunteers the opportunity to serve.

Steve's crew nicknamed him their "fearless leader" and together they accomplished many things. Here are just a few:

- Organized tailgating meals before each football game
- Established their own Facebook page
- Purchased polo shirts for the crew
- Coordinated with school administrators to have a new gate installed for access into the football stadium
- Designed and installed graphics on the band's equipment trailer
- Initiated and sponsored the purchase of an innovative new electric all terrain vehicle (ATV)

As we have seen through this example, a committee's success will rise and fall with the competency and dedication of its leader. It is critical to fill each role with the right leader. Let's take a look at some attributes that made Steve so effective in his role. These attributes apply to all committee chairs, regardless of the committee's area of focus:

1. **Enthusiasm for the extracurricular program.** You've gotta love it! Passion for the program and the desire to see students succeed is an absolute must. Enthusiasm and passion drive the committee chair's effectiveness.

2. **Interpersonal skills.** This is key. Committee chairs are on the front lines with your parent volunteers. Also, they are often the first in the booster organization to interact with parents on a personal level.

3. **Organizational skills.** Committee chairs manage the fine point details for the majority of booster activities and events. Their planning ensures that events come off without a hitch.

4. **Specialized knowledge and/or experience in the field.** Get to know your parents and their hobbies, interests, and vocations, then recruit them into the leadership roles where they fit the best. For example, our Concert Committee required specialized skills, so we recruited – and were fortunate to find – a committee chair with practical experience in lighting and sound systems.

Empower Committee Chairs to Serve to Their Full Potential

Once you match the right people to the right leadership roles, empower them to do their best, and get out of their way. Give them room to be creative. After all, they are volunteering their time and they are passionate about the program! I learned an important lesson about empowering committee chairs in my first year as president. The nation was coming out of the economic crisis of 2009, and we had delayed as many purchases as possible until things seemed to be more stable. Carol was our awesome Merchandising Committee chair, and she worked with a local vendor each year to create promotional T-shirts that we sold to our families and fans. Merchandising was not a fundraiser for us – we sold everything at cost to maximize publicity for the program. At the beginning of the year, Carol designed new graphics and was ready to place an order with her vendor. Although the funds would later be reimbursed through shirt sales, I was reluctant to approve the purchase. By putting off the purchase, I did not empower Carol to manage her committee, and I denied her the opportunity to serve. Once I realized this, I quickly approved the purchase and saw my role from a much different perspective. A major part of my role was to allow others to serve by empowering them to do their very best.

Get Off to a Great Start

At the beginning of each school year, make sure that your committee chairs know the basic guidelines and expectations of their roles. A good way to do this is by issuing them an instruction package. In this package, include guidelines for financial transactions and general leadership expectations. Along with the package, attach pertinent resources they will need. Here are a few:

- A committee chair roster
- A booster meeting and newsletter distribution schedule
- A state sales tax exemption letter
- A receipt template for all purchases.

Here's an example:

Blaze Band Boosters

July 23, 2012

Blaze Band Booster Committee Chairs,

Excitement is in the air as the Blaze Band kicks off the 2012/2013 school year! Our innovative excellence in music education is reflected in our slogan for the year, **_Blaze Band: Feel the Fire!_** As we prepare to support our directors and student musicians, I ask that you review and apply the following general guidelines to your committee activities.

Financial Transactions

- *Please ensure that all committee expenditures are approved by the booster officers in advance of a purchase.*

- *Before making approved purchases, obtain a check for the expenditure from our Treasurer. Please do not pay for items out of pocket (our accountant advises against reimbursements).*

- *When purchasing items on behalf of the band, please take advantage of our sales tax exemption status. A sales tax exemption form is provided with this letter.*

- *Receipts are required for ALL purchases.*

- *After making a purchase, please complete and attach a receipt form to the receipt and submit to the blue box as soon as possible. A receipt form is provided with this letter.*

- *When in doubt, "over-document" – provide as much information as possible regarding purpose, date, vendor, etc. for each purchase.*

- *For those making purchases with a Sam's card, document all transactions as if you are keeping a checking account register – deposits (money loaded onto the card), purchases, and dates of all transactions.*

General Committee Operations

- *Identify and develop an "understudy" that will succeed you as committee chair in future years.*

- *Document your committee activities to ensure a smooth transition to the future committee chair.*

Blaze Band Boosters

○ Create a list of the people serving on your committee, with their contact information, and share with booster officers.

○ Help assimilate new families into the program by assigning tasks to all volunteers.

○ Be present at each booster meeting, or ensure committee representation by sending a delegate. Please be prepared to provide a brief summary of current committee activities during booster meetings.

Thank you so much for your willingness to serve the Blaze Band as a committee chair! I look forward to working with you throughout the year in this great program!

Dan Caldwell, President
Blaze Band Boosters

ATTACHMENTS

2012~2013 Committee Chair Roster
2012~2013 Booster Meeting / Newsletter Distribution Schedule
State of Tennessee Sales Tax Exemption Form
Blaze Band Receipt Form

In summary, a committee's success will rise and fall with the competency and dedication of its leader. There are four major attributes of an effective committee chair: enthusiasm for the extracurricular program, interpersonal skills, organizational skills, and specialized knowledge and/or experience in the field. Once you match the right people to the right leadership roles, support and empower them and give them the opportunity to serve to their full potential.

Leadership Essential #32: Empower committee chairs to serve to their full potential.

THIRTY

Welcome New Volunteers with Hospitality

Do you know the secret of sustaining a dynamic and thriving booster organization? The one thing that will keep volunteers actively engaged year after year? The answer is actually very simple: cordially welcome new volunteers with enthusiasm and hospitality. Volunteer labor is the power to run your operation, so it is critical to continually integrate new people into the organization.

Committees provide the point of entry for new volunteers to plug into the organization. Committee volunteers are typically "on the front lines," interfacing with students, parents, and fundraising customers. Some of your new volunteers will eventually become committee chairs and officers. Therefore, be intentional in making new volunteers feel right at home.

Welcoming new volunteers is essential in maintaining a culture of acceptance. There are three major steps to assimilate new volunteers into your organization: recruit new volunteers, put them to work, and show gratitude for their efforts. Let's take a detailed look at the attributes of each step.

Recruit New Volunteers

1. **Always encourage new people to participate.**
   Regardless of your current number of volunteers, there's always room for one more. Remember, a

booster organization is dynamic, with people rotating in and out each year. Never give the impression that someone's help is not needed.

2. **Clearly define "what" it is you need people to do.** People are more likely to volunteer for a specific task than an unclear, open-ended request for help. To set expectations, communicate not only what the job entails, but also applicable school or booster rules.

3. **Give an estimated time required to do the task.** Parents of teenagers have many priorities competing for their time. If you want to increase your participation rate, provide an accurate estimate of the time required to do the task. Open-ended requests without time estimates turn people off.

4. **Call everyone who signs up to help.** Many organizations have a committee fair or other sign-up activity at the beginning of the year. When it comes time for committees to do their work, be sure to call everyone who signed up. If you don't, they will remember that they signed up and will likely feel excluded.

Put Them to Work

1. **Introduce yourself and others to new volunteers.** This sounds way too simple, but we adults often become bashful when we're around people we don't know. Be intentional in breaking the ice. A simple introduction goes a long way to make people feel welcomed and accepted.

2. **Have your current volunteers extend a welcoming hand.** When new people show up to volunteer, don't make them insert themselves into the operation. Strike up a conversation and welcome them in. Never tell a new volunteer that she is not needed, regardless of how many people you already have on the job. Take advantage of the opportunity to train someone new.

3. **Don't allow cliques to take over.** Cliques are divisive and devastating to an organization. They may start harmlessly, with a few people taking care of a task they feel they have mastered. But if you don't allow new people to take part, you won't be able to sustain the task for long. Always be on the lookout for the formation of cliques, and take swift action to break them up before they infect the organization.

4. **Train on the job.** Match new volunteers with experienced people to teach them their assigned tasks. This is especially important when working fundraisers requiring specialized skills, such as food preparation for concessions.

Show Gratitude for Their Efforts

1. **Thank them for their efforts.** Again, this is simple, yet easily overlooked. Don't miss the opportunity to convert a first-time volunteer to a regular contributor.

2. **Respect their time.** Do everything you can to release volunteers within the time you had

estimated. Remember, time is one of the most valued resources for parents of teenagers.

3. **Let them know how their participation impacts the extracurricular program and the organization.** Everyone wants to feel as if his or her contribution is useful and helpful. Be specific in letting volunteers know exactly how their work helps the organization meet its overall goals.

4. **Ask for their ideas to do things better.** New volunteers will have ideas to help you continuously improve and become more efficient. In the Blaze Band Boosters, it seemed that every year we would reach new levels that could not be outdone. However, we always found better ways of doing things in the following year that pushed us to new heights.

5. **Welcome their ideas.** Don't just ask new volunteers for their ideas; actually implement them! Never tell someone, "we've tried that before," or "that will never work." We once had a committee chair who thought her way was the only way. She was pushy and belittled the ideas of others. The situation got so bad that executive leadership had to step in because we were losing volunteers. Once we cleared that roadblock, we were able to implement innovative new ideas that advanced the way we did business.

Committee chairs have the additional responsibility to sustain the momentum as they rotate out of the organization. Here are three important tasks, taken from the committee chair instruction package:

1. **Identify and develop an apprentice who will serve as committee chair in future years.** Remember, the ideal condition is to appoint an apprentice to assume committee leadership in the future. This will allow the apprentice to participate in the activities he or she will assume when the current leader rotates out.

2. **Document committee activities to ensure a smooth transition to the future committee chair.** Although you may spend time training a successor on the job, nothing takes the place of written instructions. Over time, people are likely to forget some of what they have learned. Documented procedures are invaluable in maintaining consistent operations year after year.

3. **Create a list of the people serving on each committee, with their contact information.** It is difficult for the executive team to know where every volunteer serves. This contact list will help the team recognize people for their service. It will also help to populate the recruiting pool of future leaders.

To recap, volunteer labor is the power to run your organization. Therefore, welcoming new volunteers is critical in sustaining momentum year after year. Follow three major steps to assimilate new people into your organization: recruit new volunteers, put them to work, and show gratitude for their efforts.

Leadership Essential #33: Welcome new volunteers with enthusiasm and hospitality to sustain momentum year after year.

THIRTY-ONE

Purchase with Prudence

In most booster organizations, committee chairs make a significant number of purchases. Therefore, it is critical that everyone understands what is expected when buying things for the organization. Establish guidelines for purchases and communicate them to your committee chairs as soon as they step into their roles. These are the guidelines that I set for committee chair purchases in the Blaze Band Boosters:

1. **Approach every purchase with a frugal mindset.** This is the overarching principle when making purchases. A good rule of thumb is to spend the organization's money as if it were your own. Shop around and get competitive bids. You may find vendors willing to discount their products for school organizations. Some vendors may also offer discounts in exchange for advertising at your games or events.

2. **Get executive team approval prior to making a purchase.** When finances are tight, have the executive team review and approve all purchases. Be careful, though, not to hinder your committee chairs in the process. You may choose to allow them to spend up to their budget limits without seeking approval. For any unbudgeted spending, be sure to follow your organization's approval guidelines. Most organizations have a threshold for unbudgeted

expenditures that requires approval by vote of the booster membership.

3. **Purchase with a booster check.** Prior to making a purchase, have the buyer request a booster check from the treasurer made out to the appropriate vendor for the purchase amount. This will protect the organization against theft and fraud. It will also protect the person making the purchase from any suspicion of wrongdoing.

4. **Never buy things out-of-pocket and request a reimbursement later.** This is a poor business practice for a nonprofit organization. It contributes to impulse buying and increases the potential for purchases with lost receipts.

5. **Don't pay sales tax.** Most states extend the benefit of sales tax exemption to nonprofit organizations. To make a tax-exempt purchase, the buyer is required to present the vendor a copy of the organization's Certificate of Exemption, which is issued by the state's Department of Revenue. To take full advantage of this benefit, issue every committee chair a copy of the certificate and make sure they understand how to use it.

6. **Require receipts for all purchases.** This is a stumbling block for many organizations. Passionate committee chairs often focus on the tasks at hand and misplace their receipts. However, receipts are as important to the buyer as they are to the organization. Receipts protect buyers by proving that transactions were made. They also protect the organization by documenting where funds have

been spent. Ask your accountant how long you should retain receipts for audit purposes.

7. **When in doubt, over document.** Your bookkeeper has to match each purchase to its budgeted line item. To help with this process, gather as much information as possible from your buyers. Give them a form to report pertinent information, including the committee name, vendor, and purpose for the purchase. When buying multiple items, list them separately and indicate each item's purpose. Here's an example form:

PLEASE ATTACH THIS FORM TO ALL RECEIPTS

Name of person making the purchase	Dan Caldwell
Committee name	Band Camp Care
Check number	7526
Vendor	Walmart
Date of purchase	July 15, 2012

ITEMIZE ITEMS PURCHASED

Item purchased	Purpose	Cost
Paper cups	Band camp	$89.96
Powdered sports drink	Band camp	$458.00
Bottled water	After-school practice	$199.50

additional room on the back...

---

8. **Keep detailed records for prepaid cards.** If you use store gift cards for repetitive purchases, document each purchase separately. For example, a gift card to a warehouse club may be reloaded with funds several times to continually purchase supplies for your organization. Record all transactions as you would for a checking account, complete with deposits, purchases, and dates for each.

These eight guidelines give you some best practices when buying things for your organization. Communicate them to your committee chairs early in the year, and make sure that everyone understands the organization's expectations. With everyone "on the same page," your organization will benefit from prudent, cost effective purchases.

Leadership Essential #34: Purchase with prudence as if the organization's money were your own.

THIRTY-TWO

Create Committees to Achieve New Initiatives

In this section, we have seen the power of committees in accomplishing critical booster tasks. By their nature, committees allow the organization's work to be divided among small groups of enthusiastic volunteers. With a specific focus, committees apply their volunteers' common interests and skills to meet the organization's varying needs.

While many booster tasks remain the same from year to year, new opportunities will occasionally arise. Sometimes a new opportunity just does not fit within any current committee's scope. In this case, the most effective way to take advantage of the opportunity is to create a new committee.

Before you create new committees, be sure that your governing documents authorize you to do so. For example, your Constitution and Bylaws should include an article defining the responsibilities and expectations of committees. This article will probably list the organization's standing committees, and it should include the clause, "other committees may exist as determined by the Officers." If you don't find this clause, take the necessary steps to add it in. Chances are you'll assemble new committees regardless of your Constitution and Bylaws, so this amendment will reflect your actual process in the event of an audit.

As a point of reference, here are the Blaze Band Booster's standing committees:

- Band Camp Care
- Banquet
- Bus Chaperones
- Concert
- Forms
- Fundraising*
- Hospitality
- Merchandising
- Office Assistants
- Trip
- Truck & Equipment
- Uniforms
- Video/Photo

> *Various fundraising committees shall be established to meet the financial needs of the organization.*

These committees cover a booster organization's basic needs, and your committees are probably structured similarly. The most important consideration is to establish and align committees to best meet your program's needs.

When Should Booster Organizations Create New Committees?

How will you know when to establish a new committee? What indicators point to the need for a new team to capitalize on an opportunity? Although every opportunity is different and unique, here are four examples for new committees:

1. **When your instructor spends a considerable amount of time on non-instructional tasks.** The Blaze Band takes a spring trip every year. In the program's early years, the band directors took care of all the tasks related to travel. A few years ago, we established a trip committee to relieve the directors of this duty. Now, parent volunteers coordinate with the tour company, register students, make chaperone, room, and bus assignments, and oversee chaperone activities. This committee also provides an added benefit for the directors and the organization. It maintains an "arm's length" distance between the directors and the students' travel funds.

2. **When there is a short-term need that falls outside of a standing committee's scope.** When we transitioned to a general fund financial structure, we needed a dedicated team to focus on this specific task. We established a transition committee to interface with our parents and students, our fundraising partners, and school administrators. Within three months, the transition was complete and the committee's work was done.

   Temporary committees provide a great opportunity to develop future leaders. The Transition Committee chair was a faithful volunteer who had asked to lead with increased responsibility. She excelled in this role, and was elected treasurer the following year.

3. **When you need to train someone new.** In the Executive Leader section, we discussed the Blaze Band Boosters' ad hoc Finance Committee. Through

succession planning, we recognized that our treasurer was scheduled to "graduate" out of the program, and our bookkeeper was considering her option to rotate out as well. A full year before their potential departures, we recruited a volunteer with an accounting background to serve on a temporary committee of one, the Finance Committee. In this role, she worked alongside both financial officers and learned the organization's financial processes. The following year, she was elected treasurer, and was fully prepared for the role. And, we were fortunate to keep the current bookkeeper in the organization for another year.

4. **When the scope or volume of work exceeds the reasonable expectation of one committee chair.** A good example is fundraising. Fundraising is vital to the program, so be sure not to overload your Fundraising Committee chairs. Give them time to apply their full focus and energy toward accomplishing their fundraising goals. We had five fundraising committees. One was dedicated to our partnership with our NFL team, staffing merchandise booths. Another took care of our partnership with two local universities, staffing concession stands. We dedicated two committees to product sales (fruit and a regional coupon book). Finally, we had a committee oversee our participation in a grocery store's gift card program.

To recap, committees can effectively serve your organization by focusing your parents' skills and efforts toward a specific task or goal. It is important, though, to appropriately align your committees to best meet your program's needs. New committees often offer the best solution to address new opportunities. You'll not only be able to take advantage of new opportunities, you'll prepare future leaders in the process.

Leadership Essential #35: Create committees to achieve new initiatives.

PART SIX

LEAD YOUR LEGACY

THIRTY-THREE

Assess the Health of Your Organization

Wow! We've taken quite a journey to get here. Now it's time to get started. Time to take that first step toward leading your own thriving booster organization. But with so many things to consider, you may wonder, *where do I start?*

When every new executive team takes office, the most important first step is to assess the health of the organization. Are there any glaring issues that need to be addressed? Are there any risks that may be hidden below the surface? If so, what are the nature and extent of those risks?

In this chapter, we'll take a look at twenty-nine risks that may jeopardize your organization if not properly addressed. The severity of each ranges from a devastating risk to a special consideration. I hope you'll be able to answer "yes" to each of these conditions.

Devastating Risks

A devastating risk is a condition that may shut down your organization and result in penalties or fines. If you cannot answer "yes" to all five conditions, start immediately – today – to correct the situation. My recommendation is to seek the guidance of a qualified attorney and/or accountant.

- **The organization is registered as an IRS 501(c)(3).** Every booster organization should register as a nonprofit and claim tax exemption. While some organizations may technically fall outside of the requirement to register, it's just not worth the risk of operating in noncompliance. The IRS does not consider ignorance of the law as a valid excuse to not register.

- **The organization operates with one general fund – no student accounts.** The IRS is very clear – a booster organization may not allocate funding in a manner that benefits any individual student over other students in the program. All incoming funds must go into the general fund, and all outgoing expenses must be paid out of the fund.
- **Students are not credited for hours worked or dollars brought into the organization.** This is considered a form of individual student accounts. Funding must be distributed equally to all students, regardless of their individual participation in fundraising activities.
- **Students are not denied participation if they don't make student payments or fundraise.** Likewise, instructors cannot associate a grade with fundraising or hold a student's grades for not participating in fundraising activities.
- **The organization filed an income tax return (form 990) within the past year.** Organizations that do not file tax returns for three consecutive years automatically lose their tax exemption status. You can check your tax-exempt status online through the IRS's *Exempt Organization Select Check*[57] website.

Significant Risks

A significant risk is a condition that may result in financial loss. This could be from theft or fraud, or from liability that you are not insured against. If you cannot answer "yes" to all fourteen conditions, put together a plan to resolve the issue(s) within the next three months. And, as noted above, seek the guidance of a qualified professional if you are uncertain about any issue.

- **The organization's state charter (incorporating the organization as a legal entity) is current for the year.** This is required for your IRS tax filing, so be sure that you know when your charter comes up for renewal.
- **The organization has its own bank account.** A carefully selected bank will partner with and protect the organization from potential theft and fraud.
- **The organization has a "no cash" policy.** Eliminate the insecurity of cash transactions by instituting a "no cash" policy. You'll also eliminate the temptation for theft in the process.
- **The organization has enough "cash on hand" to begin the year.** In many organizations, a majority of expenses come at the beginning of the school year. Plan ahead so you will have the means to cover them.
- **Only current officers are authorized on the organization's bank account.** A newly elected executive team should promptly transition authority for signing booster checks. Remember, your banker will require a copy of the minutes that document

officer elections before making changes to your account.

- **Two signatures are required to authorize a booster check.** Ask your bank not to clear a check against your account without two signatures.
- **Instructors are not authorized to sign booster checks.** Instructors should maintain an "arm's length" distance from booster funds.
- **There is documentation for every dollar that comes into the organization and every dollar that goes out.** This is a sound accounting practice. Financial records "tell the organization's story" for the period in question. If you are audited, the auditor will ask to see financial records first.
- **Financial duties are split between two officers.** You will dramatically reduce your exposure to theft and fraud by segregating duties between two officers. Typical roles are treasurer and bookkeeper.
- **Monthly financial reports are provided to the executive team, parents, and school administrators.** Transparency in financial reporting makes it difficult for someone to misappropriate funds for their own personal gain.
- **Fundraisers comply with state sales tax exemption laws.** Most states allow nonprofit organizations to conduct fundraisers without charging their customers sales tax, but there are usually restrictions. Specifically, be sure you know how many sales you may conduct without charging sales tax, and the duration allowed for each sale.

- **There is a secure deposit box in the classroom or locker room.** This simply keeps everyone honest.
- **The organization has insurance on trailers and equipment.** Don't leave home without it.
- **The organization has general liability insurance if serving concessions.** This will protect you from a customer's claim or lawsuit.

Considerable Risks

A considerable risk is a condition that may impact your organization's ability to support its extracurricular program. This could be due to a lack of volunteer participation or inaccurate planning and budgeting. If you cannot answer "yes" to all seven conditions, work to resolve the issue(s) as quickly as possible. If you allow one of these conditions to linger, you may suffer from lost opportunity.

- **An annual kick-off meeting is scheduled, including a committee fair.** From day one, recruit new families and find how they best fit in serving the organization.
- **All committee chair positions are filled before the annual kick-off meeting.** Committee chairs are the primary point of contact in recruiting new volunteers. A committee without a chair will miss the opportunity to reach new people.
- **The parent body is unified – no cliques.** Nothing will take down an organization faster than cliques. They are distracting, disruptive, and

divisive. Be proactive in creating unity within the organization, and don't allow cliques to take hold.

- **A formal budget has been developed and shared with school administrators.** Your budget is the financial roadmap for the organization. If your school administrators do not require a copy of your budget, create good will by providing them a copy.
- **The budget is achievable and will meet the program's needs.** Run a quick "back of the napkin" calculation to be sure that all your program's needs are accounted for within the year's budget.
- **Scheduled fundraisers are capable of providing enough income to run the program.** Again, quickly estimate the expected proceeds for each fundraiser to be sure they will meet the program's needs. Do this early in the year so you can modify your fundraising plan if necessary.
- **The organization keeps a Certified Public Accountant on retainer.** A CPA will guide you through the year's financial events, audit your books, and assist with tax and legal filings. Additionally, a CPA will provide you peace of mind that far exceeds the fees you will spend on her services.

Special Considerations

A special consideration is a best practice that will contribute to your organization's overall success. If you can answer "yes" to these three conditions, you have the breadth of volunteers who, with proper leadership, will help the organization thrive.

- **The financial officers have a background in accounting or bookkeeping.** Nothing takes the place of hands-on experience, especially in an area as critical as finance.
- **Officers chair no more than one committee (in addition to their elected office).** It is not uncommon for officers to chair committees. It is sometimes in the organization's best interest for an officer to chair a committee, as it gives the committee an executive sponsor. However, it is not healthy for a small core group to lead the majority of the organization's activities.
- **Each committee chair leads only one committee.** Provide many people the opportunity to serve. On the surface, it may seem difficult to recruit enough volunteers to fill all positions without doubling up. However, your persistence in recruiting will pay dividends when it is time for succession planning.

Well, how'd you do? I hope that you were able to answer "yes" to all of these conditions. If so, you are taking over a well-run organization. You can begin to focus on bigger things, like advancing the program over the midterm. If you uncovered some issues, don't be discouraged. Now you know the risks before you, and you can begin to turn things around. Remember to seek the guidance of a qualified professional when necessary, and reflect back on the prior chapters for specific instruction along the way.

THIRTY-FOUR

Execute Your Plan

Do something worth remembering.

– Elvis Presley

Dr. Steven R. Covey revolutionized the way many Americans approach personal growth with his best selling book, *The Seven Habits of Highly Effective People.*[58] Habit 3, First Things First, made popular the concept of the urgent vs. the important. By Dr. Covey's definitions, urgent tasks have a deadline associated with them. Important tasks, on the other hand, contribute to your mission. The premise is all too familiar – don't overcommit to the urgent at the expense of the important.

As the parent of a teenager, you've likely never been busier than you are now. And, as a volunteer leader, you're living the delicate balance between the urgent and the important. You're prioritizing work and other pressing commitments against family time and volunteering. Chances are you've become very efficient at managing your time. But what happens when you can't fit it all in?

Do Something Significant

I recently heard New York Times best selling author Rory Vaden on the Chris LoCurto podcast.[59] In the interview, Rory introduced a third dimension, beyond the urgent and the important – the *significant*. When you cannot fit everything into your day, you may feel a sense of guilt. Because of this, Rory says that "time management is not a logical issue, it is an emotional issue." Significance, therefore, addresses the emotional aspect of time management. In measuring significance, ask yourself, how long will this activity or decision affect the course of events into the future? Keeping this in perspective, you can allocate your time without guilt. As a booster leader, you have the chance to do something significant, to influence hundreds of young lives in the program you serve. The time you spend today will impact this generation for years to come. Sadly, very few people take the opportunity to do something this significant in their entire lifetime.

We are all busy, and we sometimes feel as if we cannot fit anything else into our schedule. It is easy to become overcommitted, partially because many of us struggle with saying no. Rory suggests, "You think you have a hard time saying no, but you don't. When you say yes to one thing, you are saying no to something else." Thinking in terms of significance, the "something else" may be a number of other priorities that may long benefit from your time and attention.

Your child's teenage years are a fleeting moment in time. Invest your time now in the significant. Sure, there will be other things that you'll have to turn down in the process, but that's only temporary. The time you spend serving your child's booster organization is an investment you'll never regret.

Cast Your Vision and Develop Your Plan

In many ways, leading a booster organization is like running a small business. Engaged, intentional leaders drive the success of each. These great leaders cast their vision, develop a plan to achieve that vision, and carry out their plan to realize achievements of tremendous significance.

Great leaders invest their time in others and cultivate relationships to develop more great leaders. They understand that they cannot run their organization alone. Only with the combined, cohesive efforts of many will their vision be achieved. Therefore, great leaders create an atmosphere of teamwork and they motivate others to do their best.

Now it's your turn. You know what to do – after all, you've read this book! Consider each chapter as your step-by-step guide to build a thriving organization. Cast your vision and map out your plan. Set your sights clearly upon your goals, and maintain focus until they are fully achieved.

This is Your Time

I firmly believe that you have been brought to this moment for a reason. This is YOUR time. Your organization is looking to you for leadership. No one else has your responsibility. What will be your vision? When it's time to "hang up the keys," what will be your legacy?

As you begin your journey, remember not many people have the opportunity in life to do something truly amazing, but you do. You have that opportunity. You have the potential to impact the lives of the next generation. The time is now. Go forth and be AWESOME!!!

Bonus Online Resources

I have created a special bonus for *The Booster Leader* readers – an additional section, *The Booster Leader: Travel & Chaperone*.

Nearly every extracurricular program will travel at some point throughout the year. This bonus section walks you through the entire process of planning your trip, preparing for travel, and leading your group while on the road. Here you will find best practices and step-by-step instructions for a safe and enjoyable trip that will create lifelong memories.

To download your free copy, visit www.TheBoosterLeader.com/bonus. You will receive *The Booster Leader: Travel & Chaperone* when you sign-up to receive product updates and news from around *The Booster Leader* community. There is no obligation, and you may unsubscribe at any time.

Be sure to visit www.TheBoosterLeader.com often to keep up with the latest in booster leadership.

APPENDIX A

The 35 Leadership Essentials

Leadership Essential #1: The booster leader must be committed to serve the students.

Leadership Essential #2: Lead with devotion as if your financial livelihood depends on it.

Leadership Essential #3: The booster leader takes care of people and money.

Leadership Essential #4: Five attributes of the executive leader are passion, inspiration, servant leadership, transparency, and influence.

Leadership Essential #5: The executive leader delegates and allows others to serve.

Leadership Essential #6: Recruit in the zone where a person's passion intersects his or her strengths.

Leadership Essential #7: Recognition is the greatest motivator available to the executive leader.

Leadership Essential #8: Unity must be a priority and is accomplished through intentional leadership.

Leadership Essential #9: A comprehensive annual calendar of events provides a roadmap for the executive leader.

Leadership Essential #10: The prudent leader casts a vision for the future and strives to achieve that vision throughout the midterm.

Leadership Essential #11: The executive leader guides the executive team and facilitates their discussion to ensure success.

Leadership Essential #12: Decisions made by consensus foster unity among the executive team.

Leadership Essential #13: Booster meetings are the executive leader's opportunity to energize the core group of volunteers.

Leadership Essential #14: Succession planning enables the organization to sustain the momentum through the transition of leadership.

Leadership Essential #15: A booster organization must distribute funds equally to all students, regardless of their individual participation in fundraising activities.

Leadership Essential #16: No student may be denied the opportunity to participate in an extracurricular program based on his or her ability to participate in fundraising.

Leadership Essential #17: Transparent operating procedures are the foundation of a booster organization's financial integrity.

Leadership Essential #18: Separate financial roles and reporting between two or more people.

Leadership Essential #19: Partner with your bank to prevent internal and external theft and fraud.

Leadership Essential #20: A comprehensive, accurate budget serves as the financial roadmap for the organization.

Leadership Essential #21: Organizations may request but not require student payments.

Leadership Essential #22: To meet your fundraising goals, provide value and service to your customer.

Leadership Essential #23: The frugal leader effectively meets every need at the lowest possible cost.

Leadership Essential #24: Assess the risks to your organization and carry insurance to reduce those risks.

Leadership Essential #25: Communicate financial status clearly and in a timely manner.

Leadership Essential #26: Compelling internal and external communications are vital to an organization's livelihood.

Leadership Essential #27: Clear, concise, and timely reminders will increase attendance and participation in your organization's events.

Leadership Essential #28: A booster organization that operates with integrity maintains accurate meeting minutes.

Leadership Essential #29: A thriving booster organization publishes impactful newsletters on a consistent basis.

Leadership Essential #30: Use social media to engage your organization's members.

Leadership Essential #31: Develop and execute a strategy to promote and build the brand of your program.

Leadership Essential #32: Empower committee chairs to serve to their full potential.

Leadership Essential #33: Welcome new volunteers with enthusiasm and hospitality to sustain momentum year after year.

Leadership Essential #34: Purchase with prudence as if the organization's money were your own.

Leadership Essential #35: Create committees to achieve new initiatives.

APPENDIX B

The Blaze Band Story

In the fall of 1998, all eyes across the state of Tennessee were focused on the University of Tennessee's football team. Peyton Manning had just departed to the Indianapolis Colts, and the Volunteers seemed an unlikely candidate for success. To most of the nation's surprise, the Vols went on a winning streak, racking up an undefeated season and a trip to the national championship game. In the Fiesta Bowl, the Vols defeated Florida State University and brought home their first national championship since 1951.

For many middle Tennesseans, that was the extent of our exposure to Florida State. However, something was happening at Florida State that would forever impact the lives of many of our high school students for years to come. Brenda Monson and Billy Stepp were pursuing advanced degrees in music. They studied research and personal philosophies to create a strong band program that would provide a healthy and successful musical experience for their future students. Structured similar to a college band, the band would be entertaining and fun, but with an acute focus on the music.

In response to a booming population growth in Murfreesboro, Tennessee, Blackman High School was constructed and opened its doors in the fall of 2000. Brenda and Billy were selected to be the inaugural band directors. Taking this opportunity to launch their concept, the Blaze Band was born.

In the Blaze Band, music is considered an integral fabric of the human experience.[60] In addition to creating aesthetically pleasing experiences, music gives the students a glimpse of culture and history. With a holistic view of music's influence, character and integrity are woven into the program's core values. Students are as likely to be instructed, "it's not what you get, it's what you give"[61] as they are in the rhythm and timing of the current song they are learning.

Many great musicians have come up through the Blaze Band, but there is a deeper understanding that not everyone will continue their pursuit of music education beyond high school. The Blaze Band offers something for every student and fosters the creation of lifelong friendships. I witnessed this culture of acceptance first hand through my children's experiences. Upon entering the program as freshmen, they were immediately welcomed and accepted by upperclassmen. This was just the opposite of my own high school band experience some thirty years prior. There was an understood rank and order, and freshmen were expected to "pay their dues."

The centerpiece of the Blaze Band is its football band. Notice that I didn't say "marching band," but "football band." Yes, the band marches during the halftime show, but their contribution to the overall Friday night game experience far exceeds simply "marching." The Blaze Band does not compete in marching competitions. This allows the flexibility to perform fun and entertaining halftime shows, featuring the music of Michael Jackson, the Doobie Brothers, and Earth, Wind, and Fire to name a few.

Students have created the tradition of doing the Hokey Pokey, followed by the cheer, "It's Showtime!" before taking the field. At halftime, the band runs onto the field, dances to some of their numbers, and ends every performance with the school fight song. The band has had its own dedicated press box announcer who builds excitement leading into the halftime show. A student rock band keeps things lively during game time, playing classic rock and roll (while the football team is playing defense, of course). In the stands, band members are always on their feet, cheering on the team and building excitement with their repertoire of adrenaline pumping tunes.

The Blaze Band is serious about the music. Nearly all of the football band preparations and rehearsals are done outside of normal classroom time. From day one, the band focuses on concert music. By the end of September, when most high school bands are gearing up for marching contests, the Blaze Band performs its first concert. Often, a professor from a local university conducts some of the numbers, giving the students an amazing opportunity to learn beyond their high school level.

At Christmas, the band performs its PRISM concert, a non-stop, wall-to-wall array of music and special lighting effects. Here's how it works – as one of the concert bands finishes a number on stage, an ensemble will begin to play from a back corner of the auditorium, followed by a jazz band performance up front, and so on. The show culminates with football band members lining the perimeter of the auditorium to perform the football halftime show music one more time. The audience's experience in the vortex of sound is simply amazing.

The winter concert highlights the students' innovations. Some musical numbers accompany a video for a synchronized sight and sound experience – a crowd favorite. In the spring, students show their mastery of the music for the year's final concert. The performance often features songs that students wrote or arranged.

Specialty bands round out the Blaze Band. The Rock Band, Jazz Bands, and Percussion Ensembles offer students the opportunity to expand their scope into music of different genres. Percussion ensembles create some of the greatest innovations in sound. Here are a few "instruments" you're likely to hear: newspapers, cardboard boxes, paper sacks, garbage cans, plastic totes and buckets, PVC pipes filled with gravel, ladders, brooms, and basketballs!

Through the years, continuous improvements and a few minor changes have been made, but the core program that was created at Florida State remains. Brenda Monson serves as Senior Director, but Billy Stepp left a few years back to become Principal at another school. Hundreds of young lives – and many adults' lives – have been enriched through the Blaze Band. I sincerely thank Brenda Monson for providing this awesome learning opportunity for our students at Blackman High School.

ABOUT THE AUTHOR

Dan Caldwell is the trusted authority on booster leadership. He has led student support organizations for nearly two decades. He served the Blackman High School Band Boosters for eight years in roles of increasing responsibility: volunteer, chaperone, committee chair, vice president, and president. For twelve years, he served in a variety of leadership roles with the Boy Scouts of America as his son pursued and achieved the rank of Eagle scout.

Professionally, he leads a creative team that delivers innovative solutions for a Fortune Global 50 company. Dan is certified by Toastmasters International as a Competent Communicator.

Dan and his wife, Katrina, have two children, Grant and Katelyn. They live in Murfreesboro, Tennessee, just outside of Nashville.

NOTES

[1] John Maxwell, Developing the Leader Within You (Nashville, TN: Thomas Nelson, 1993), x.

[2] *Elvis* and *Elvis Presley* are registered trademarks of Elvis Presley Enterprises, Inc., Memphis, TN.

[3] Chuck Baril, *Nashville Elvis*, http://nashvilleelvis.com.

[4] Elvis Presley, *Blue Suede Shoes*. Carl Perkins. © 1956 by RCA. 45 RPM.

[5] Jon Acuff, *Start: Punch Fear in the Face, Escape Average and Do Work that Matters* (Brentwood, TN: Lampo Press, 2013), eBook edition.

[6] Simon Sinek, *Start with Why: How Great Leaders Inspire Everyone to Take Action* (New York: Penguin Group, 2009).

[7] Jennifer McMurrer, Center on Education Policy. *Choices, Changes, and Challenges: Curriculum and Instruction in the NCLB Era* (Washington, D.C.: December 2007).

[8] "Intention," Dictionary.com Unabridged. Random House, Inc. http://dictionary.reference.com/browse/intention (accessed: August 26, 2013).

[9] "Lead," Dictionary.com Unabridged. Random House, Inc. http://dictionary.reference.com/browse/lead (accessed: August 26, 2013).

[10] Bob Morris. "Robert Steven Kaplan: An Interview by Bob Morris." June 25, 2013. http://bobmorris.biz/robert-steven-kaplan-an-interview-by-bob-morris.

[11] Board of Education, State of Tennessee, *Rules of the State Board of Education, Chapter 0520-1-3, Minimum Requirements for the Approval of Public Schools,* January 30, 2009, Nashville, Tennessee.

[12] Jim Collins, *Good to Great* (New York: HarperCollins Publishers, 2001).

[13] *The Andy Griffith Show*, "One-Punch Opie," CBS, December 31, 1962, written by Harvey Bullock.

[14] Dave Ramsey, *EntreLeadership* (New York: Howard Books, 2011), eBook edition.

[15] Chris McChesney, Sean Covey, Jim Huling, *The 4 Disciplines of Execution* (New York: Free Press, 2012), 24-25.

[16] Jeff Sandvig, "School Support Organizations, Rutherford County Schools" (Materials presented at the annual school support organization meeting, Murfreesboro, Tennessee, August 31, 2010).

[17] Dropbox (cloud-based file storage resource), www.dropbox.com (accessed October 12, 2013).

[18] The Official Robert's Rules of Order Web Site, www.robertsrules.com/history.html (accessed September 15, 2013).

[19] Wikipedia contributors, "Consensus decision making," Wikipedia, The Free Encyclopedia, http://en.wikipedia.org/w/index.php?title=Consensus_decision-making&oldid=570641121 (accessed September 16, 2013).

[20] "Consensus," Merriam-Webster.com, http://www.merriam-webster.com/dictionary/consensus (accessed September 16, 2013).

[21] Wikipedia contributors, "Groupthink," Wikipedia, The Free Encyclopedia, http://en.wikipedia.org/w/index.php?title=Groupthink&oldid=5725 67392 (accessed September 16, 2013).

[22] Christopher Avery, "How Consensus Decision Making Creates Shared Direction in a Team," Christopher Avery & The Leadership Gift (blog), September 20, 2011, http://christopheravery.com/blog/how-consensus-decision-making-creates-shared-direction-in-a-team (accessed September 16, 2013).

[23] U.S. Department of the Treasury, Internal Revenue Service, Exemption Requirements – Section 501(c)(3) Organizations, (Washington, DC: 2013), http://www.irs.gov/Charities-&-Non-Profits/Charitable-Organizations/Exemption-Requirements-Section-501(c)(3)-Organizations (accessed September 24, 2013).

[24] "Inure," Dictionary.com Unabridged. Random House, Inc. http://dictionary.reference.com/browse/inure (accessed: September 24, 2013).

[25] Valarie Honeycutt Spears. "Audits Trouble Bryan Station Baseball boosters." Kentucky.com. http://www.kentucky.com/2008/12/16/628251/audits-trouble-bryan-station-high.html (accessed September 24, 2013).

[26] U.S. Department of the Treasury, Internal Revenue Service, Life Cycle of a Public Charity, (Washington, DC: 2013), http://www.irs.gov/Charities-&-Non-Profits/Charitable-Organizations/Life-Cycle-of-a-Public-Charity (accessed September 26, 2013).

[27] U.S. Department of the Treasury, Internal Revenue Service, Exemption Requirements – Section 501(c)(3) Organizations, (Washington, DC: 2013), http://www.irs.gov/Charities-&-Non-Profits/Charitable-Organizations/Exemption-Requirements-Section-501(c)(3)-Organizations (accessed September 24, 2013).

[28] U.S. Department of the Treasury, Internal Revenue Service, Life Cycle of a Public Charity – Jeopardizing Exemption, (Washington, DC: 2013), hhttp://www.irs.gov/Charities-&-Non-Profits/Charitable-Organizations/Life-Cycle-of-a-Public-Charity-Jeopardizing-Exemption (accessed September 26, 2013).

[29] Barton Deiters. "Lowell sports booster treasurer admits to embezzling and agrees to repay club." *mLIVE.com*. http://www.mlive.com/news/grand-rapids/index.ssf/2011/10/lowell_sports_booster_treasure.html (accessed September 30, 2013).

[30] Lauren Steussy. "Volunteer admits to embezzling $50,000 from Costa Mesa High School band." *Orange County Register*. http://www.ocregister.com/articles/band-527274-borders-piatti.html (accessed September 30, 2013).

[31] Felicia Krieg. "Booster Club treasurer admits embezzlement." *Press Republican*. http://pressrepublican.com/0100_news/x1413935231/Booster-Club-treasurer-admits-embezzlement (accessed September 30, 2013).

[32] Patricia Schaefer. "Employee Theft: Identify and Prevent Fraud, Embezzlement, Pilfering, and Abuse." *Business Know-How*. http://www.businessknowhow.com/manage/employee-theft.htm (accessed October 1, 2013).

[33] Bill Hybels. *Character: Who You Are When No One's Looking* (Downers Grove, IL: InterVarsity Press, 1994).

[34] "Separation of Duties," BusinessDictionary.com. WebFinance, Inc. http://www.businessdictionary.com/definition/separation-of-duties.html (accessed: September 27, 2013).

[35] Intuit QuickBooks (accounting software for small business), www.quickbooks.intuit.com (accessed October 12, 2013).

[36] Wikipedia contributors, "Fidelity bond," Wikipedia, The Free Encyclopedia, http://en.wikipedia.org/w/index.php?title=Fidelity_bondoldid=574609182 (accessed October 12, 2013).

[37] Dropbox (cloud-based file storage resource), www.dropbox.com (accessed October 12, 2013).

[38] PayPal (global e-commerce business), www.paypal.com (accessed October 14, 2013).

[39] Tennessee Secretary of State, Rules of the State Board of Education – Chapter 0520-01-03-.03 (14) (b) 2. School Fees, (Nashville, TN: 2013), http://www.tn.gov/sos/rules/0520/0520-01/0520-01-03.20130729.pdf (accessed October 15, 2013).

[40] An attorney with nonprofit specialization approved the term "student payment."

[41] Wikipedia contributors, "Fidelity bond," Wikipedia, The Free Encyclopedia, http://en.wikipedia.org/w/index.php?title=Fidelity_bond&oldid=574609182 (accessed October 30, 2013).

[42] Wikipedia contributors, "Umbrella insurance," Wikipedia, The Free Encyclopedia, http://en.wikipedia.org/w/index.php?title=Umbrella_insurance&oldid=567051814 (accessed October 30, 2013).

[43] Google Gmail (email provider), www.mail.google.com (accessed November 10, 2013).

[44] Yahoo! Mail (email provider), www.mail.yahoo.com (accessed November 10, 2013).

[45] One Call Now (voice and text blast provider), www.onecallnow.com (accessed November 10, 2013).

[46] Office.com (Microsoft Office resource center), http://office.microsoft.com (accessed November 19, 2013).

[47] Andreas M. Kaplan, Michael Haenlein, "The early bird catches the news: Nine things you should know about micro-blogging," *Business Horizons* 54 (2011): 2.

[48] Wikipedia contributors, "Twitter," Wikipedia, The Free Encyclopedia, http://en.wikipedia.org/w/index.php?title=Twitter&oldid=582398042 (accessed November 20, 2013).

[49] "What is a media sharing site?" *Affilorama*. http://www.affilorama.com/internet101/media-sharing (accessed November 20, 2013).

[50] Wikipedia contributors, "YouTube," Wikipedia, The Free Encyclopedia,

http://en.wikipedia.org/w/index.php?title=YouTube&oldid=582566 954 (accessed November 20, 2013).

[51] "Social Media." *Mashable.* http://www.mashable.com/category/social-networking (accessed November 20, 2013).

[52] "Number of Active Users at Facebook Over the Years," *Associated Press.* http://bigstory.ap.org/article/number-active-users-facebook-over-years-5 (last modified May 1, 2013).

[53] Wikipedia contributors, "Value proposition," Wikipedia, The Free Encyclopedia, http://en.wikipedia.org/w/index.php?title=Value_proposition&oldid =573787151 (accessed November 24, 2013).

[54] Tennessee Department of Education, Graduation Requirements, (Nashville, TN: 2013), http://www.tn.gov/education/gradreq.shtml (accessed November 24, 2013).

[55] Samantha E. Williams, "Blaze Band drummer doesn't miss a beat," *Daily News Journal,* September 3, 2011. Samantha E. Williams, "When Blackman high band marches, this drummer rolls," *The Tennessean,* September 4, 2011.

[56] Joseph Pleasant, "Mother helps son realize dream of joining marching band," *WKRN-TV Nashville.* September 16, 2011. http://www.wkrn.com/story/15484515/mother-helps-sons-dream-of-joining-marching-band-possible?clienttype=printable (accessed November 24, 2103).

[57] U.S. Department of the Treasury, Internal Revenue Service, EO Select Check, (Washington, DC: 2013), http://www.irs.gov/Charities-&-Non-Profits/Exempt-Organizations-Select-Check (accessed December 10, 2013).

[58] Dr. Stephen R. Covey, *The Seven Habits of Highly Effective People* (New York: Free Press, 1989).

[59] Chris LoCurto, *Procrastinate on Purpose with Rory Vaden,* podcast audio, The Chris LoCurto Show, MP3, 32:21. Accessed December 12, 2013. http://chrislocurto.com/procrastinate-on-purpose-with-rory-vaden-podcast/.

[60] Blackman High School Band. Blackman Blaze Band Handbook. http://www.blackmanband.com/news/Band%20Forms/BHS%20Band%20Handbook.pdf (accessed December 13, 2013).

[61] Scott Lang, Scott Lang Leadership Seminars. http://www.scottlang.net (accessed February 16, 2014).

91140350R00153

Made in the USA
San Bernardino, CA
17 October 2018